AwareKnits™

AwareKnits™

Knit & Crochet Projects for the Eco-Conscious Stitcher

Vickie Howell and Adrienne Armstrong

LARK BOOKS

A Division of Sterling Publishing Co., Inc.
New York / London

SENIOR EDITOR
Valerie Van Arsdale Shrader

EDITOR
Nathalie Mornu

ART DIRECTOR
Kristi Pfeffer

ILLUSTRATOR
Orrin Lundgren

PHOTOGRAPHER
Scott Jones

COVER DESIGNER
Chris Bryant

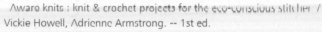
Library of Congress Cataloging-in-Publication Data

Aware knits : knit & crochet projects for the eco-conscious stitcher /
Vickie Howell, Adrienne Armstrong. -- 1st ed.
      p. cm.
   Includes bibliographical references and index.
   1. Knitting--Patterns. 2. Crocheting--Patterns. I. Howell, Vickie. II.
Title.
   TT825.A75 2009
   746.43'2041--dc22

                                    2008054384

10 9 8 7 6 5 4 3 2 1

First Edition

Published by Lark Books, A Division of
Sterling Publishing Co., Inc.
387 Park Avenue South, New York, NY 10016

Text © 2009, Vickie Howell and Adrienne Armstrong
Photography © 2009, Lark Books, A Division of
Sterling Publishing Co., Inc.; unless otherwise specified
Illustrations © 2009, Lark Books, A Division of
Sterling Publishing Co., Inc.

Distributed in Canada by Sterling Publishing,
c/o Canadian Manda Group, 165 Dufferin Street
Toronto, Ontario, Canada M6K 3H6

Distributed in the United Kingdom by GMC Distribution Services,
Castle Place, 166 High Street, Lewes, East Sussex, England BN7 1XU

Distributed in Australia by Capricorn Link (Australia) Pty Ltd.,
P.O. Box 704, Windsor, NSW 2756 Australia

If you have questions or comments about this book, please contact:
Lark Books
67 Broadway
Asheville, NC 28801
828-253-0467

Manufactured in China

ISBN 13: 978-1-60059-469-4

For information about custom editions, special sales, and premium and corporate purchases, please
contact the Sterling Special Sales Department at 800-805-5489 or specialsales@sterlingpub.com.

 This book was printed on recycled paper with agri-based inks.

To our beautiful boys, who inspire us daily to lead balanced, peaceful, and mindful lives.

Introduction

Nowadays, environmental consciousness isn't just about recycling plastic bottles and refusing to drive a gas-guzzling car. It's a way of life—a way of thinking about life and making choices to help create a better world. As a stitcher, you've already taken a humble step in the right direction: you choose to create instead of consume, and to use simple resources to practical effect. Yay for you!

Now, as far as greening up your stitching, we're not suggesting you rid your stash of every piece of acrylic or rayon in sight. To us, that would be like giving up carbs. (Seriously, how do people do that!?) Truth be told, the only real way to guarantee that a yarn is 100 percent green is by organically raising the crop or animal on your own farm, then harvesting efficiently and humanely, processing without the use of chemicals, spinning, and naturally dyeing the fiber yourself. We don't know about you, but with families, jobs, and, well, *lives*, that's not a reality for us.

What is realistic, though, is making an effort to know where our supplies come from so that we can make informed choices. All of the projects you'll find in this book fall under the "sustainable" umbrella for one of the following reasons:

- The source material comes from a crop that is consistently in abundance and therefore easily regenerated: jute, soy, bamboo, hemp, etc.
- The wool comes from animals that were raised organically and humanely: baby alpaca, baby camel, merino sheep, etc.
- The "yarn" was created by recycling and repurposing otherwise disposable objects: T-shirts, newspaper, plastic bags, and unwanted sweaters.
- The production and sale of the yarn supports and benefits the livelihood of independent people or communities: co-ops, artisans, and nonprofits.

We learned a lot about sustainability while we were working on this book together. Because we're in different time zones, we chatted on our computers and did mad emailing and texting back and forth as we did research. We shared our info with one another, organized it, applied it to the book, and now we want to share it with you, too. 'Cause knowledge is power, you know?

At the same time, we understand that not everything works for everybody. For example, Adrienne drives a hybrid car and buys organic. Vickie chooses a vegetarian lifestyle and focuses on recycling. We both support local wool farms, spinners, and green companies whenever we can. These are the choices that work for us. Throughout the book, we offer you some tips about eco-friendly living that are related to knitted or crocheted projects (oh yes, there are 31 great garments or accessories made from all these sustainable yarns, too). These are designed to help you make conscious decisions about your crafting and your life.

Poke around in your own eco-conscience, and see what fits your lifestyle. For us, it's about doing what we can, and doing what feels right. You may not be able to put every eco-tip into practice, but we hope you come away with a greater awareness of sustainable stitching, and that you try something new along the way. Being mindful of your stitching imprint is a new kind of eco-consciousness; it's an *AwareKnits*™!

—Vickie and Adrienne

 Vickie:
It's cool that we could share our research and work together virtually since we live half a country away from each other!

 Adrienne:
Absolutely. Technology is a beautiful thing.

Terms of Awareness

Sustainable (sə-stān-ə-bəl\) adj.: a: of, relating to, or being a method of harvesting or using a resource so that the resource is not depleted or permanently damaged <sustainable techniques> <sustainable agriculture> b: of or relating to a lifestyle involving the use of sustainable methods <sustainable society>. —Merriam-Webster.com

Green (grēn) n.: A supporter of a social and political movement that espouses global environmental protection, bioregionalism, social responsibility, and nonviolence. —FreeDictionary.com

Eco-friendly (eekow`frendlee) adj.: Not damaging to the environment, or directed at preventing environmental damage. —WordWebOnline.com

For the Body

Having an environmental conscience doesn't mean giving up on fashion. In this section, you'll find cool garments and accessories to knit up for kids, men, and women, from scarves and hats to cardis, skinny ties, and socks. With these stitched projects, it's so easy being green.

Alpaca fiber does your body good. Soft and cozy, without the bulk of a full-length scarf, our neck-warming scarflet is the perfect size to pair with a coat.

Skill Level ⭐

Size
One Size Fits All

Finished Measurements
4½ x 41½"/11 x 105cm

Materials and Tools
Blue Sky Alpacas Bulky Natural (50% wool, 50% alpaca; 3.5oz/100g = 45yd/41m): 2 skeins, color Brown Bear #1006—approx 90yd/82m of superbulky weight yarn, ⑥

Knitting needles: 10mm (size 15 U.S.) or size to obtain gauge

Tapestry needle

1 button, 1"/3cm diameter

Sewing needle and thread

Gauge
8 sts and 10 rows = 4"/10cm in St st

Always take time to check your gauge.

Instructions

CO 9 sts.

Rows 1–6: Work in garter st.

Rows 7–10: Work in St st.

Rep Rows 1–10 until piece measures 32"/81cm, ending with Row 10.

Next row (RS): K4, yo, k2tog, knit to end (buttonhole made).

Next row: Purl.

Continue to work Rows 1–10 of pat, starting with Row 7, until piece measures 41½"/105cm, ending with Row 6. BO.

FINISHING
Weave in ends. Line up button at the center of Row 23, and sew in place.

Vickie:
Adrienne, what's your favorite thing about alpaca?

Adrienne:
I love that it's super soft and that the undyed colors are all SO beautiful!

A Big Softie

Alpaca is a wonderfully soft, versatile fiber that comes in gorgeous colors naturally. It's one of our favorite fibers because not only is it luxurious to work with, but it's also lanolin-free, which means no chemical washing is necessary.

Be a Slacker: Don't Go the Extra Mile

When you can, buy organic yarn from a local farm. Buying locally means cutting out the fuel used to transport yarn cross-country. Organic + Zero Fuel = win-win, people.

FOR THE BODY

Polar Cap

We're big fans of the trusty cardi—especially one with cap sleeves! Our eco-glam version has a little sustainable sparkle lent by a metallic and soysilk yarn. The top-down construction allows you to try it on as you knit, while the lace panels offer subtle waist shaping. Come for the sweater, stay for the soy.

Skill Level

Size
Women's S (M, L, XL, XXL)

Finished Measurements
Bust: 34 (38, 42, 46, 50)"/86 (97, 107, 117, 127)cm

Length: 21½ (23, 24½, 26, 27½)"/55 (58, 62, 66, 70)cm

Materials and Tools
SWTC/Vickie Howell Collection Vegas (67% wool, 29% Soysilk, 4% Lurex; 1.75oz/50g = 109yd/99m): 6 (7, 8, 9, 10) skeins, color Cirque #420 (shown on page 17) or Casino #418—approx 654 (763, 872, 981, 1090)yd/594 (693, 792, 891, 990)m of worsted weight yarn, (4)

Knitting needles: 5.5mm (size 9 U.S.) 24"/61cm circular and dpns or size to obtain gauge

Stitch markers

Stitch holders or waste yarn

Tapestry needle

7 buttons, 1"/3cm in diameter

Sewing needle and thread

Gauge
16 sts and 20 rows = 4"/10cm in St st

Always take time to check your gauge.

Stitch Pattern
Fishtail Lace Panel:

Row 1 (RS): P1, k1, yo, k2, sl1-k2tog-psso, k2, yo, k1, p1.

Row 2: K1, p9, k1.

Row 3: P1, k2, yo, k1, sl1-k2tog-psso, k1, yo, k2, p1.

Row 4: Rep Row 2.

Row 5: P1, k3, yo, sl1-k2tog-psso, yo, k3, p1.

Row 6: Rep Row 2.

Instructions
Note: The cardigan is knit in one piece from the top down.

YOKE
CO 13 (14, 15, 16, 17) sts for front, pm, CO 8 (9, 10, 11, 12) sts for sleeve, pm, CO 22 (24, 26, 28, 30) sts for back, pm, CO 8 (9, 10, 11, 12) sts for sleeve, pm, CO 13 (14, 15, 16, 17) sts for other front—64 (70, 76, 82, 88) sts.

Do not join in a round, work back and forth in rows.

Work in k1, p1 rib for 1"/2.5cm, ending with a WS row.

Next row (RS): Work to 1 st before first marker, kfb, slip marker, kfb, *work to 1 st before next marker, kfb, slip marker, kfb; rep from * across (8 sts increased).

Next row: Purl.

Rep last 2 rows a total of 19 (22, 25, 28, 31) times—216 (246, 276, 306, 336) sts.

21½ (23, 24½, 26, 27½)"/55 (58, 62, 66, 70)cm

13 (13½,14, 14½, 15)"/33 (34, 36, 37)cm

34 (38, 42, 46, 50)"/86 (97, 107, 117, 127)cm

BODY

Next row (RS): K32 (36, 40, 44, 48) front sts, place next 46 (53, 60, 67, 74) sleeve sts on a holder, CO 8 sts for underarm, k60 (68, 76, 84, 92) back sts, place next 46 (53, 60, 67, 74) sleeve sts on a holder, CO 8 sts for underarm, k32 (36, 40, 44, 48) front sts. Work even in St st on 140 (156, 172, 188, 204) body sts for 2 (2½, 3, 3½, 4)"/5 (6, 8, 9, 10)cm, ending with a WS row.

Begin Fishtail Lace panels as follows:

Next row (RS): K1, pm, work 11 lace panel sts, pm, knit to last 12 sts, pm, work 11 lace panel sts, pm, k1.

Continue as established, working lace panel sts between markers, for 8½"/22cm.

Work even in St st for ½"/1cm more.

Work in k2, p2 rib for 2½"/6cm. BO loosely.

Sleeves (Make 2)

Place 46 (53, 60, 67, 74) held sleeve sts on dpns. Pick up and knit 8 sts for underarm from body underarm sts and join in a round—54 (61, 68, 75, 82) sts.

Next round: Dec 2 (1, 0, 3, 2) sts evenly around—52 (60, 68, 72, 80) sts.

Work in k2, p2 rib for 1"/3cm. BO. Rep for second sleeve.

FINISHING

Button Band

Pick up and knit 3 sts for every 4 rows along Left Front. Work in garter st for 1"/3cm. BO.

Buttonhole Band

Pick up and knit 3 sts for every 4 rows along Right Front. Work in garter st for ½"/1cm, ending with a WS row.

Next row (RS): Evenly space 7 buttonholes along row, working each buttonhole as k2tog, yo twice, ssk. Work in garter st for ½"/1cm more. BO.

Weave in ends. Sew buttons opposite buttonholes.

 Vickie:
It seems like today, pretty much anything can be made from soy—I love it!

 Adrienne:
Yeah, it's one of those progressive fibers that's amazing—if it's processed simply. Don't be afraid to ask yarn companies about their methods for turning soy into yarn so you can be informed about your purchase.

Soy Joy?

The process of transforming soy (or corn, bamboo, and other base materials) into yarn is rarely 100 percent eco-friendly. As educated, sustainable stitchers, though, we say weigh the good with the bad and make your own informed decision.

For example, soy yarn is a valuable advancement in the industry. It's made from recycling the byproduct from manufacturing tofu, thereby repurposing something that would otherwise go to waste. Soy itself is also an abundant crop and therefore a sustainable resource. On the flip side, however, the production process for turning any plant matter into yarn can often be chemically intensive, resulting in a negative impact on the air and water in the surrounding area.

The bottom line for us is that, although soy- and other plant-derived fibers may not be the glowing beacon of environmental perfection, we believe that knitting with them, or any effort to utilize sustainable, non-petroleum-based resources, is a step in the right direction toward the grand scheme of the greener good.

Fashion Slowdown

In an era of garments mass-produced for a pittance, it's important to take time to smell the fashion roses. Balance out the disposable tops and shoddily made skirts in your wardrobe with pieces that are well constructed for fair wages and with considered materials. There are clothing companies out there with a conscience; do some research and look for those that use sustainable materials (such as soy and hemp) as well as help drive employment in developing countries.

FOR THE BODY

Wrist Factor

We're huge fans of wrist warmers; they're quick to knit, make great gifts, and keep your hands warm without being cumbersome to wear. Knit up a pair of our seed-stitched version, slip them on, and turn down your thermostat to save some energy.

Skill Level ★ ★

Size
Child (Women's S/M, Men's M/L)

Finished Measurements
Stretches to fit hand circumference 7 (8, 9)"/18 (20, 23)cm

Materials and Tools
Plymouth Earth Mainland (80% baby alpaca, 20% silk; 1.75oz/50g = 71yd/65m): 2 skeins, color Charcoal #05—approx 142yd/130m of worsted weight yarn, ④

Knitting needles: 4.5mm (size 7 U.S.) dpns or size to obtain gauge

Tapestry needle

Gauge
18 sts and 28 rows = 4"/10cm in seed st

Always take time to check your gauge.

Instructions (Make 2)
CO 28 (32, 36) sts, divide evenly onto 3–4 dpns. Join, taking care not to twist the sts.

Work in k2, p2 rib for 3 (4, 4)"/8 (10, 10)cm.

Work in seed st until piece measures 5 (6, 7)"/13 (15, 18)cm from edge.

THUMB OPENING
Continue in seed st, working back and forth in rows, for 1 (1¼, 1½)"/3 (3, 4)cm.

Change back to knitting in the round—this will close the top of the thumb slit—and work in seed stitch for an additional 1 (1½, 2)"/3 (4, 5)cm.

Work last 2 rounds in garter st. BO.

FINISHING
Weave in ends.

Vickie:
I never used to remember to turn my computer off, but our research has me more conscious about doing it. I admit it's still a work in progress for me to change that habit.

Adrienne:
Yeah, it's surprising how much energy can be saved with the push of one little button.

What a Turnoff

Besides turning down the thermostat, you can also save energy by turning your computer off. It's been reported that leaving your computer on can cost you a bunch of extra money in energy bills every year—enough that you could afford an additional latte every week. Leaving it on 24/7 also dumps 1,500 pounds (680.4 kG) of CO_2 into the atmosphere. It takes anywhere from 100 to 500 trees to absorb enough carbon dioxide to offset the emissions of that one computer if it's on all the time. So save the planet (and some change) while you sleep tonight by turning your computer off before you turn out the lights.

Wristy Business

Knitting and crochet can take a toll on your wrists and hands, so it's important to baby them a bit as you're working. Every 20 minutes or so, set down your project, rotate your wrists in circles, and then stretch each one as follows.

1. Stretch your right arm out in front of you with the palm facing down.

2. With your left hand, press the fingers of your right hand back, toward your arm.

3. Stretch your left hand in the same manner.

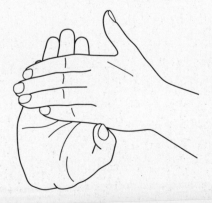

Pash-Greena

Pash-Greena

Ditch those worthless, paper-thin blankets supplied by the airlines in favor of a little luxury! Our delicious travel wrap soothes the soul and warms the body during life's adventures. Besides, you'll be amazed how a little cruelty-free cashmere will soften the blow of another grueling, food-free flight!

Skill Level ★ ★ ★

Size
One Size Fits All

Finished Measurements
23 x 72"/58 x 183cm

Materials and Tools
Cape Cod Fibers Lobster Pot Aran Weight Cashmere (100% cashmere; 1.75oz/50g = 100yd/91m): 12 skeins, color Natural—approx 1200yd/1092m of worsted weight yarn,

Knitting needles: 5mm (size 8 U.S.) or size to obtain gauge

Stitch holder or waste yarn

Tapestry needle

Gauge
19 sts and 21 rows = 4"/10 cm in pat st
Always take time to check your gauge.

Pattern Stitch

Lace
Row 1 (RS): P2, *yo, k4, sl1-k2tog-psso, k4, yo, p1; rep from *, ending with p2.

Row 2 (and all WS rows through 10): K2, p108, k2.

Row 3: P2, *k1, yo, k3, sl1-k2tog-psso, k3, yo, k1, p1; rep from *, ending with p2.

Row 5: P2, *k2, yo, k2, sl1-k2tog-psso, k2, yo, k2, p1; rep from *, ending with p2.

Row 7: P2, *k3, yo, k1, sl1-k2tog-psso, k1, yo, k3, p1; rep from *, ending with p2.

Row 9: P2, *k4, yo, sl1-k2tog-psso, yo, k4, p1; rep from *, ending with p2.

Rep Rows 1–10 for pat.

Instructions
CO 112 sts.

Rows 1–2: Knit.

Rep Rows 1–10 of Lace pat a total of 19 times or to half of desired length. Place sts on holder.

This constitutes half of the pashmina. Repeat to make the other half.

FINISHING
Graft both pieces tog using Kitchener st. Weave in ends. Block.

knit ▬
yarn over ○
purl |
sl 1-k2tog-psso ⋏

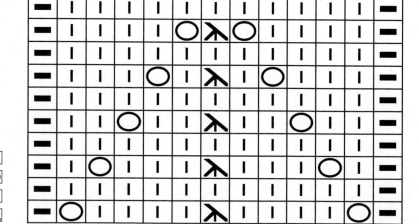

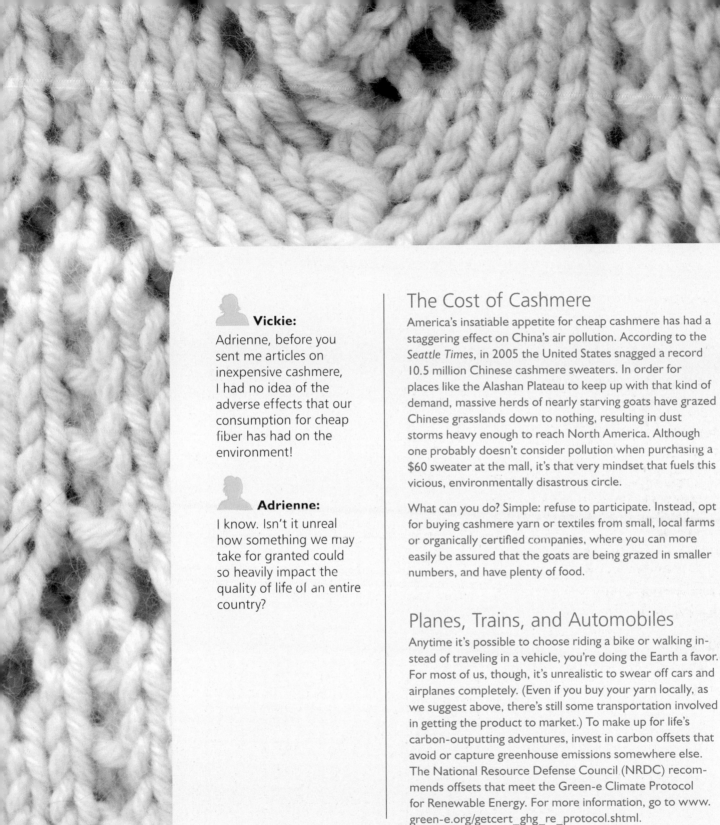

Vickie:

Adrienne, before you sent me articles on inexpensive cashmere, I had no idea of the adverse effects that our consumption for cheap fiber has had on the environment!

Adrienne:

I know. Isn't it unreal how something we may take for granted could so heavily impact the quality of life of an entire country?

The Cost of Cashmere

America's insatiable appetite for cheap cashmere has had a staggering effect on China's air pollution. According to the *Seattle Times*, in 2005 the United States snagged a record 10.5 million Chinese cashmere sweaters. In order for places like the Alashan Plateau to keep up with that kind of demand, massive herds of nearly starving goats have grazed Chinese grasslands down to nothing, resulting in dust storms heavy enough to reach North America. Although one probably doesn't consider pollution when purchasing a $60 sweater at the mall, it's that very mindset that fuels this vicious, environmentally disastrous circle.

What can you do? Simple: refuse to participate. Instead, opt for buying cashmere yarn or textiles from small, local farms or organically certified companies, where you can more easily be assured that the goats are being grazed in smaller numbers, and have plenty of food.

Planes, Trains, and Automobiles

Anytime it's possible to choose riding a bike or walking instead of traveling in a vehicle, you're doing the Earth a favor. For most of us, though, it's unrealistic to swear off cars and airplanes completely. (Even if you buy your yarn locally, as we suggest above, there's still some transportation involved in getting the product to market.) To make up for life's carbon-outputting adventures, invest in carbon offsets that avoid or capture greenhouse emissions somewhere else. The National Resource Defense Council (NRDC) recommends offsets that meet the Green-e Climate Protocol for Renewable Energy. For more information, go to www. green-e.org/getcert_ghg_re_protocol.shtml.

FOR THE BODY

Camisoul

A feminine tank top is a summer wardrobe must-have. Our version's peekaboo lace body, simple bust shaping, and delicate straps are good for a gal's figure. The organic cotton it's made from—well, that's good for the soul!

Skill Level

Size
Women's XS (S, M, L, XL)

Finished Measurements
Bust: 30 (34, 38, 42, 46)"/76 (86, 97, 107, 117)cm

Length (excluding straps): 17 (18, 19, 20, 21)"/43 (46, 48, 51, 53)cm

Materials and Tools
Blue Sky Alpacas Skinny Dyed (100% organically grown cotton; 1.75oz/50g = 150yd/137m): 4 (5, 6, 6, 7) skeins, color Squash #306—approx 600 (750, 900, 900, 1050)yd/548 (685, 822, 822, 959)m of DK weight yarn, ❸

Knitting needles: 4mm (size 6 U.S.) and 3.75mm (size 5 U.S.) or size to obtain gauge

Stitch markers

Stitch holders

Tapestry needle

Gauge
20 sts and 28 rows = 4"/10cm in St st using larger needles

Always take time to check your gauge.

Pattern Stitches

Diamond Lace
Row 1 (RS): *K1, k2tog, yo, k1, yo, ssk, k2; rep from * across.

Row 2 and all WS Rows: Purl.

Row 3: *K2tog, yo, k3, yo, ssk, k1; rep from * across.

Row 5: *Yo, k5, yo, sl1-k2tog-psso; rep from * across.

Row 7: *Yo, ssk, k3, k2tog, yo, k1; rep from * across.

Row 9: *K1, yo, ssk, k1, k2tog, yo, k2; rep from * across.

Row 11: *K2, yo, sl 1-k2tog-psso, yo, k3; rep from * across.

Row 12: Purl.

Rep Rows 1–12 for pat.

Linen Stitch
Row 1 (RS): *K1, sl1 purlwise wyif; rep from * across.

Row 2: *P1, sl1 purlwise wyib; rep from * across.

Rep Rows 1–2 for pat.

Instructions

FRONT
Using larger needles, CO 88 (96, 104, 112, 120) sts.

Work in Diamond Lace pat for 11 (111/2, 12, 121/2, 13)"/28 (29, 30, 32, 33)cm, ending with a WS row.

Shape Ribs
Using smaller needles, continue as follows:

Work in k1, p1 rib, dec 1 st each end every row until there are 70 (80, 90, 100, 110) sts. If necessary, work even in rib until ribbed portion measures 11/2"/4cm, ending with a WS row.

Shape Bust
Row 1 (RS): Change to larger needles. K19 (23, 26, 29, 33), pm, k32 (34, 38, 42, 44), pm, k19 (23, 26, 29, 33).

Row 2 (and all WS rows unless otherwise noted): Purl.

Row 3: *Knit to 1 st before marker, kfb, slip marker, kfb; rep from * once, knit to end.

Continuing in St st, rep last row twice more, every 7th row—82 (92, 102, 112, 122) sts.

Next RS row: Ssk, knit to last 2 sts, k2tog.

Continuing in St st, rep last row on RS, twice more. 76 (86, 96, 106, 116) sts. Divide sts in half, and put the last 38 (43, 48, 53, 58) sts on a holder. From here work one half of the bust at a time.

Left Bust

Dec 1 st at each end, every row until 4 sts remain.

Work 4 more rows in St st. Place sts on holder.

Right Bust

Place held sts on needle. Join yarn, rep as for left.

BACK

With larger needles, CO 88 (96, 104, 112, 120) sts.

Work in Diamond Lace pat until piece measures 11 (11½, 12, 12½, 13)"/28 (29, 30, 32, 33)cm, ending with a WS row.

Shape Ribs

Change to smaller needles. Work ribbing as for Front, working even until ribbed portion measures 3"/8cm. BO in pat.

FINISHING

Weave in ends. Block. Seam sides.

Straps (Make 2)

Place 4 rem sts from one holder on smaller needles and work strap in Linen Stitch for 10 (10½, 11, 11½, 12)"/25 (27, 28, 29, 30)cm or desired length.

(Note: Be sure to tug the strap a bit after each row, to align sts.) BO. Sew to back, at appropriate place for fit.

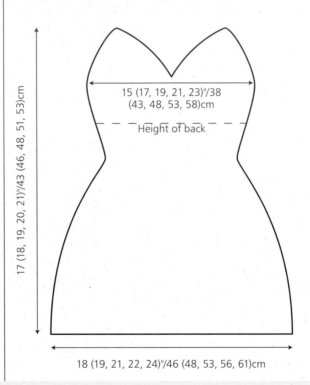

15 (17, 19, 21, 23)"/38 (43, 48, 53, 58)cm

Height of back

17 (18, 19, 20, 21)"/43 (46, 48, 51, 53)cm

18 (19, 21, 22, 24)"/46 (48, 53, 56, 61)cm

Adrienne:

Vickie, I think it's really important for us to fill people in on what makes cotton organic, and why it matters.

Vickie:

Absolutely! For me, learning about cotton was the gateway to opening my mind about other organic textiles and fibers.

What Makes Cotton Organic?

The difference between organic and nonorganic cotton breaks down fairly simply to how it's grown and the way it's processed. Cotton must meet the following standards in order to be certified organic:

* The plants can't be genetically modified.

* Crops must be planted and grown in a field that's been pesticide-free for at least three years.

* Yarn or textile processing must be free of harsh and toxic chemicals, including petroleum, silicon waxes, formaldehyde, and chlorine bleach.

Brrr is Better

Ninety percent of the energy used for washing a garment like this is spent on heating the water. Try giving your laundry the cold shoulder by avoiding washing it in hot temperatures. Your clothes will come out just as clean and you'll be twice as cool.

Solar
Sweetie

Solar Sweetie

Our sweet summer dress is perfect for any green little girl. The corn fiber it's knit from, and the stitch pattern it's knit in, shed an alternative light on old-school smocking, creating baby couture with a conscience.

Skill Level

Size

0–6 months (6–12 months, 12–18 months, 24 months)

Finished Measurements

Chest: 16 (18, 19, 20)"/41 (46, 48, 51)cm

Materials and Tools

SWTC A-Maizing (100% corn fiber; 1.75oz/50g = 130yd/118m): 2 (2, 2, 3) skeins, color Grenadine #366—approx 260 (260, 260, 390) yd/236 (236, 236, 354)m of DK weight yarn, 3️⃣

Knitting needles: 3.5mm (size 4 U.S.) straight and dpns and 4mm (size 6 U.S.) straight or size to obtain gauge

Tapestry needle

Gauge

20 sts and 28 rows = 4"/10cm in St st using larger needles

Always take time to check your gauge.

Special Abbreviations

Smocking Stitch (Sm st): Insert RH needle from front between 6th and 7th sts on LH needle and draw through a loop; keeping loop fairly snug, place it on LH needle and knit it together with first st on LH needle.

Pattern Stitch

Smocking

Rows 1 and 3 (WS): K2, *p2, k2; rep from * across.

Row 2: P2, *k2, p2; rep from * across.

Row 4: P2, *Sm st, k1, p2, k2, p2; rep from * across.

Rows 5 and 7: Rep Rows 1 and 3.

Row 6: Rep Row 2.

Row 8: P2, k2, p2, *Sm st, k1, p2, k2, p2; rep from * across, end with k2, p2.

Rep Rows 1–8 for pat.

Instructions

FRONT AND BACK (MAKE 2)

With smaller straight needles, CO 42 (58, 66, 74) sts. Work Rows 1–8 of Smocking pat 2 (2, 3, 3) times.

Next row (WS): Change to larger needles, purl.

Next row: *K2, yo; rep from * to last 2 sts, k2—62 (86, 98, 110) sts.

Work even in St st for 7½ (8½, 9½, 11)"/19 (22, 24, 28)cm, ending with a WS row.

Next row (RS): K2, *yo, k2tog; rep from * to end.

Next 2 rows: Work in St st.

Work 5 rows in garter st. BO.

STRAPS (MAKE 4)

With dpns and RS facing, pick up and knit 3 sts on one of the top edge corners of dress. Work in i-cord for 7 (8, 8½, 9)"/18 (20, 22, 23)cm. BO. yarn, leaving a 1–2"/3–5cm tail. Rep for each top corner of dress Front and Back.

FINISHING

Weave in ends. Sew side seams. Block.

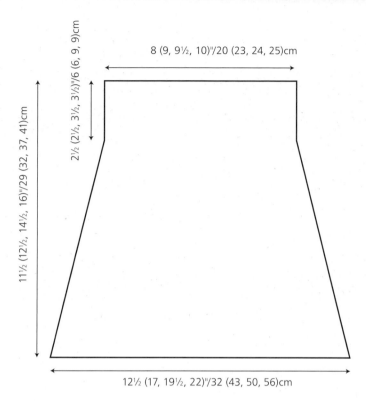

8 (9, 9½, 10)"/20 (23, 24, 25)cm

2½ (2½, 3½, 3½)"/6 (6, 9, 9)cm

11½ (12½, 14½, 16)"/29 (32, 37, 41)cm

12½ (17, 19½, 22)"/32 (43, 50, 56)cm

Adrienne:
I was really surprised to learn how reliant we are, as a society, on corn.

Vickie:
Yeah, and even stitchers can get their fix now with yarn made from corn fiber!

Wünder Corn!

No matter what your stance is on a corn-based product like ethanol, it's difficult not to be impressed by how versatile a veggie corn is, and how reliant we are on it. Did you know that about 2,500 of the products in the average grocery store use corn in some form during processing or production, including cosmetics, alcohol, cake mixes, and paper plates? A-maizing!

Screen Your Sunscreen

When your little darlin' wears this dress, you'll need to protect her skin from the sun. When you choose a sunscreen, be sure to opt for an organic, paraben-free cream. This will ensure that her delicate skin is not only protected from the sun, but also from a host of chemicals found in many sun products.

FOR THE BODY

Greensleeves

Less is more when it comes to designs for the modern guy, so we kept our men's zip-up cardigan simple, with subtle asymmetrical panels and exposed seams. This yarn is produced by a Uruguayan cooperative that strives to bring economic opportunities to rural women. Son, brother, husband—a guy in a sleek sweater with a social purpose is a guy worth knowing.

Skill Level

Size

Boys' 8 (10, 12, Men's XS, S, M, L, XL)

Finished Measurements

Chest: 28 (30, 32, 34, 38, 42, 46, 50)"/71 (76, 81, 86, 97, 107, 117, 127)cm

Length: 18 (191/2, 21, 23, 24, 25, 26, 27)"/46 (50, 53, 58, 61, 64, 66, 69)cm

Materials and Tools

Manos Del Uruguay Silk Blend (70% merino, 30% silk; 1.75oz/50g = 150yd/137m): 7 (8, 9, 10, 11, 12, 13, 14) skeins, color Olive #3055—approx 1050 (1200, 1350, 1500, 1650, 1800, 1950, 2100)yd/959 (1096, 1233, 1370, 1507, 1644, 1781, 1918)m of DK weight yarn, ③

Knitting needles: 4mm (size 6 U.S.) or size to obtain gauge

Stitch holder

Sewing thread and needle

Tapestry needle

Sewing machine (optional)

Separating zipper, approx 2"/5cm longer than sweater length

Gauge

20 sts and 28 rows = 4"/10cm

Always take time to check your gauge.

Instructions

BACK

CO 70 (74, 80, 84, 96, 104, 116, 124) sts. Work even in St st for 9 (10, 11, 12, 12½, 13, 13½, 14)"/23 (25, 28, 30, 32, 33, 34, 36)cm, ending with a WS row.
Note: Actual body length to underarm will be 3"/8cm longer once ribbing is added later.

Shape Armholes

BO 5 (6, 7, 8, 8, 8, 8, 8) sts at beg of next 2 rows—60 (62, 66, 68, 80, 88, 100, 108) sts.
Work even in St st for 6 (6½, 7, 8, 8½, 9, 9½, 10)"/15 (17, 18, 20, 22, 23, 24, 25)cm more, ending with a WS row.

Shape Shoulders

BO 4 (4, 4, 4, 6, 8, 8, 8) sts at beg of next 4 rows—44 (46, 50, 52, 56, 56, 68, 76) sts.
BO 4 (4, 4, 5, 5, 5, 8, 8) sts at beg of next 2 rows.

BO 5 sts at beg of next 2 rows—26 (28, 32, 32, 36, 36, 42, 50) sts.
Place rem back neck sts on holder.

RIGHT FRONT PANEL I

CO 18 (20, 22, 26, 30, 36, 42, 46) sts.

Row 1 (RS): K3, p2, knit to end.

Row 2: Purl to last 5 sts, k2, p3.

Rep last 2 rows for 5 (5½, 6, 6½, 7, 7½, 8, 8½)"/13 (14, 15, 17, 18, 19, 20, 22)cm.

Next row (RS): K3, p2, knit to last st, M1, k1.

Next row: Purl to last 5 sts, k2, p3.

Rep last 2 rows 15 more times—34 (36, 38, 42, 46, 52, 58, 62) sts.

Next row (RS): K3, p2, knit to end.

Next row: Purl to last 5 sts, k2, p3.

Rep last 2 rows until piece measures 9 (10, 11, 12, 12½, 13, 13½, 14)"/23 (25, 28, 30, 32, 33, 34, 36)cm, ending with a RS row.

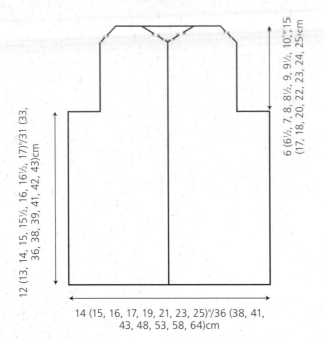

12 (13, 14, 15, 15½, 16, 16½, 17)"/31 (33, 36, 38, 39, 41, 42, 43)cm

14 (15, 16, 17, 19, 21, 23, 25)"/36 (38, 41, 43, 48, 53, 58, 64)cm

6 (6½, 7, 8, 8½, 9, 9½, 10)"/15 (17, 18, 20, 22, 23, 24, 25)cm

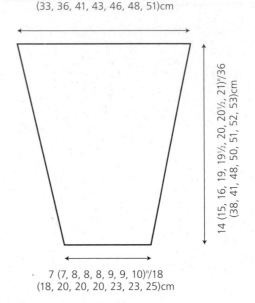

12 (13, 14, 16, 17, 18, 19, 20)"/31 (33, 36, 41, 43, 46, 48, 51)cm

14 (15, 16, 19, 19½, 20, 20½, 21)"/36 (38, 41, 48, 50, 51, 52, 53)cm

7 (7, 8, 8, 8, 9, 9, 10)"/18 (18, 20, 20, 20, 23, 23, 25)cm

Shape Armhole

BO 5 (6, 7, 8, 8, 8, 8, 8) sts at beg of next WS row, work in pat to end—29 (30, 31, 34, 38, 44, 50, 54) sts.

Work even in St st, maintaining k3, p2 rib at edge, for 4 (4½, 5, 6, 6½, 7, 7½, 8)"/10 (11, 13, 15, 17, 18, 19, 20)cm more, ending with a WS row.

Shape Neck and Shoulder

Row 1 (RS): BO 2 (3, 4, 6, 6, 8, 11, 15) sts, knit to end.

Row 2: Purl.

Continuing in St st, dec 1 st at neck edge of every RS row 10 times.

At the same time, when piece measures 6 (6½, 7, 8, 8½, 9, 9½, 10)"/15 (17, 18, 20, 22, 23, 24, 25) cm from armhole, begin shoulder shaping as follows:

BO 4 (4, 4, 4, 6, 8, 8, 8) sts at beg of next 2 WS rows.

BO 4 (4, 4, 5, 5, 5, 8, 8) sts at beg of next WS row.

BO 5 sts at beg of next WS row.

RIGHT FRONT PANEL 2

CO 45 (47, 49, 51, 53, 55, 57, 59) sts.

Row 1 (RS): Knit to last 2 sts, k2tog.

Row 2: Purl.

Rep last 2 rows 12 more times—32 (34, 36, 38, 40, 42, 44, 46) sts. BO.

LEFT FRONT PANELS 1 AND 2

Work panels as for Right Front, reversing shaping.

SLEEVES (MAKE 2)

CO 36 (36, 40, 40, 40, 44, 44, 48) sts. Work in k2, p2 rib for 3"/8cm.

Work in St st, inc 1 st each end of row every 4th row until there are 60 (65, 70, 80, 85, 90, 95, 100) sts. Work even until piece measures 14 (15, 16, 19, 19½, 20, 20½, 21)"/36 (38, 41, 48, 50, 51, 52, 53) cm from beg. BO.

FINISHING

Block. Sew each Front Panel 2 to corresponding Front Panel 1, seaming with WS held tog to make seam show on RS. Sew shoulder seams. Attach sleeves, sew side and sleeve seams.

Waistband

Pick up and knit 140 (150, 160, 170, 190, 210, 230, 250) sts around bottom edge of sweater. Work in k2, p3 rib for 3"/8cm. BO.

Neck Band

Pick up 50 (55, 60, 65, 75, 80, 85, 90) sts around neck edge, including held neck sts. Work in k2, p3 rib for 3"/8cm. BO.

Weave in ends.

Machine- or hand-stitch zipper onto jacket opening.

 Vickie:

Back in the day, sweaters like this were almost always sent to the dry cleaner. And it's a very toxic process. But we know that it's not always feasible for everyone to completely cut out dry cleaning from their lives...

 Adrienne:

No, it's not, especially if you have to dress for success in your work. However, it's important for people to seek out healthier options and also to request safer methods from local dry cleaners.

Greener Cleaner

The toxic solvent perchloroethylene (perc), used in dry cleaning, is known to cause headaches, nausea, and dizziness. It has been linked to reproductive problems in both men and women, and has been labeled by the International Agency for Research in Cancer as a human carcinogen. Oh, and it ain't so great for the air you're breathing, either! Go green with your clean, and, whenever possible, steer clear of garments labeled "Dry clean only."

If home-washing all of your clothes isn't realistic (and for those of you out there with office jobs, we totally get it), look for "wet cleaning" options, which are harmless to your clothes and significantly safer for both your body and your planet.

Clean Enough?

For garments that you absolutely have to dry clean, you can lessen the impact of the process by simply doing it, well, *less*. To protect sweaters from perspiration, consider wearing a lightweight tank or tee underneath. You can also refresh dry-cleanable garments in the dryer, using a low heat setting; toss in a damp towel and a sachet to steam and freshen. Lastly, a home steamer or an iron with a steaming function can also help cut down on trips to the dry cleaner; the heat and steam will add a breath of fresh air.

FOR THE BODY

Capelet Crusader

Lightweight, feminine, and versatile—capelets are one of our favorite ways to gussy up an otherwise boring outfit. Our version's made in black to keep it classic, with paper linen to make it modern, and combined with bamboo and silk to give it drape. Crochet one for yourself because, after all, every activist needs a cape(let).

Skill Level ★★

Size

One Size Fits All

Finished Measurements

23 x 40"/58 x 102cm

Materials and Tools

SWTC/Vickie Howell Collection Love (30% silk, 70% bamboo; 1.75oz/50g = 99yd/90m): 5 skeins, color June & Johnny #255—approx 495yd/450m of worsted weight yarn,

Habu A-60 "Shosenshi" Paper (100% linen; 1.75oz/50g = 280yd/255m): 2 skeins, color Sumi Black #119—approx 560yd/510m of lace weight yarn, ⓪

Crochet hook: 5.5mm (size I U.S.) or size to obtain gauge

Tapestry needle

Gauge

12 sts and 5 rows = 4"/10cm in pat st

Always take time to check your gauge.

Instructions

TOP PANEL

With both yarns held tog, ch 53.

Row 1: Dc in 3rd ch from hook and across. Turn—51 sts.

Row 2: Ch 3, dc in next dc and across. Turn.

Row 3: Ch 3, dc2tog, dc to last 3, dc2tog, DC. Turn.

Rep last row 4 more times—41 sts. Fasten off.

MAIN BODY

Row 1 (RS). With RS facing, and starting at upper LH edge, ch 12, work sc as follows: 14 sc down side 1, 2 sc at corner, 36 sc across bottom, 2 sc at corner, 14 sc up side 2, ch 15. Turn.

Row 2: Dc in 3rd ch from hook and across, working dc in each sc and ch. Turn—92 sts.

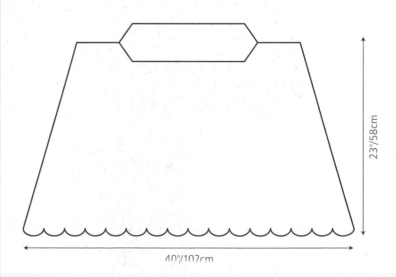

Row 3: Ch 4, skip 2, *8 tr in next st, skip 3, sc, ch 9, skip 3, sc, skip 3; rep from * 6 more times, 8 tr in next st, skip 3, sc. Turn.

Row 4: Ch 6, skip 1 tr, sc in next tr, ch 9, skip 4 tr, sc in next tr, skip 1 tr and 1 sc, *8 tr in 5th ch of ch-9 sp, skip 1 sc and 1 tr, sc in next tr, skip 1 tr and 1 sc; rep from * 6 more times, skip 1 tr, sc in ch-4 sp. Turn.

Row 5: Ch 4, *8 tr in 4th ch of ch-9 sp, skip 1 sc and 1 tr, sc in next tr, ch 9, skip 4 tr, sc in next tr, skip 1 tr and 1 sc; rep from * 6 more times, skip 1 tr and 1 sc, 8 tr in 5th ch of ch-9 sp, sc in ch-6 sp. Turn.

Rep Rows 4 and 5 seven more times and Row 4 once more after that. Fasten off.

FINISHING

Edging and Ties

With RS facing, join yarns at lower RH corner. Sc evenly along side of capelet; at top corner, ch for 18"/46cm (or desired tie length). Turn.

Sc in 2nd ch from hook and in every ch, sc along top edge evenly; at opposite corner, ch for 18"/46cm (or desired tie length).

Flip ch over to work on underside, sc in 2nd ch from hook and in every ch, sc evenly along 2nd side of capelet. Fasten off.

Weave in ends. Let hang to shape.

 Vickie:
Bamboo seems to be the alternative fiber source du jour, but there's a lot to know about it before jumping on the bamboo wagon.

 Adrienne:
Yeah, you and I've had lengthy conversations about this, because there's definitely two sides to the eco-coin here.

The Scoop on Bamboo

Bamboo is perhaps our planet's most sustainable resource. It grows fast—up to a foot a day!—and is ready to harvest in four years. It doesn't require replanting because of its complex root systems. The environmentally safe way of processing bamboo into yarn involves machine crushing the woody parts of the plant, then using enzymes to break the bamboo into mush so the fibers can be mechanically combed out and spun into yarn. This process is fairly costly and labor-intensive, but it doesn't pollute the air or have the same health risks associated with it as its multiphase, chemical-processing cousin.

Buy Indie!

Ever see a paper linen accessory at your local discount store? Didn't think so. Supporting local artists and independent businesses is one way to take a stand against the large carbon imprint of big-box stores, the common practice of purchasing from sweatshops by certain multibillion dollar chains, and the cheap quality of products often found in large, retail outlets. Try searching out boutiques and craft fairs in your own community, or jump online to sites like Etsy.com and BuyOlympia.com, virtual market places filled with handmade indie wares!

FOR THE BODY

Cloud Cover

Lightweight and delicate, these are the perfect accessories to stash in your bag when you need just a little bit of extra warmth. The baby merino wool will surround you with soft, luxurious goodness. If you've never knit lace before but always wanted to try, this project, lovies, is for you.

Skill Level ★ ★ ★

Size
One Size Fits All

Finished Measurements
Scarf: 7½ x 60"/19 x 152cm, after blocking

Arm Warmers: 7"/18cm long, after blocking

Materials and Tools
Malabrigo Lace (100% baby merino wool; 1.75oz/50g = 470yd/428m): 3 skeins, color Charrua #259—approx 1410yd/1284m of lace weight yarn,

Knitting needles: 4mm (size 6 U.S.) or size to obtain gauge

Tapestry needle

Gauge
32 sts and 32 rows = 4"/10cm in garter st

Always take time to check your gauge.

Pattern Stitch

DROPPING ELM LACE

Row 1 (RS): *K1, yo, k1, ssk, p1, k2tog, k1, yo, p1, ssk, p1, k2tog, yo, k1, yo; rep from * to last st, k1.

Row 2: P1, *p4, k1, p1, k1, p3, k1, p4; rep from * across.

Row 3: *K1, yo, k1, ssk, p1, k2tog, k1, p1, sl1-k2tog-psso, yo, k3, yo; rep from * to last st, k1.

Row 4: P1, *p6, k1, p2, k1, p4; rep from * across.

Row 5: *[K1, yo] twice, ssk, p1, [k2tog] twice, yo, k5, yo; rep from * to last st, k1.

Row 6: P1, *p7, k1, p1, k1, p5; rep from * across.

Row 7: *K1, yo, k3, yo, sl1-k2tog-psso, p1, yo, k1, ssk, p1, k2tog, k1, yo; rep from * to last st, k1.

Row 8: P1, *[p3, k1] twice, p7; rep from * across.

Row 9: *K1, yo, k5, yo, ssk, k1, ssk, p1, k2tog, k1, yo; rep from * to last st, k1.

Row 10: P1, *p3, k1, p2, k1, p8; rep from * across.

Rep Rows 1–10 for pat.

Instructions

SCARF
CO 69 sts.

Rows 1–6: Knit.

Begin Dropping Elm Lace pat, beg and ending each row with k4 throughout. Continue as established until piece measures 59½"/151cm from beg.

Knit 6 rows. BO. Block scarf before picking up sts for hood.

HOOD
Pick up and knit 219 sts evenly across edge of scarf, centered along side, beg approx 20"/51cm from end. Begin Dropping Elm Lace pat, beg and ending each row with k4 throughout. Continue as established until piece measures 12"/30cm. BO loosely.

Fold hood in half and seam top together. Weave in ends.

Arm Warmers (Make 2)
CO 61.
Rows 1–12: *K1, p1; end k1.
Begin Dropping Elm Lace pat, work even until piece measures 6"/15cm. Rep Rows 1–12 once more. BO.

FINISHING
Block. Seam up back. Weave in ends.

Vickie:
Truth be told, I'm having a hard time giving up all of my favorite chemical-based products. Slowly, though, I'm finding more and more options that I can happily live with.

Adrienne:
Me, too. We're really lucky, because there are SO many more options available now, more than there were even a few years ago.

No Chemical Attraction

Take your first step toward chemical freedom by ridding your house of personal care and cosmetic items that contain anything you can't pronounce. If you're not sure whether what you've got is good or not, check the labels to see if any of the following ingredients are listed. If so, consider ditching them for a greener way.

1. Parabens—with ethyl, methyl, butyl, or propyl as the prefix, they're linked to weight gain, hormone disruption, and breast cancer.

2. Fragrance—it's easy to pronounce but still no bueno because it's often just a cover-up term for phthalates, which are linked to liver damage and birth defects.

3. Triclosan—an unnecessary antibacterial agent that's a known irritant.

4. Petrochemicals—listed as sodium lauryl sulfate (SLS), polyethylene glycol (PEG, PPG, cocoate), propylene glycol, or artificial colors, these are derived from oil, which is a finite resource.

5. Coal tar—found in hair dyes, listed as FD&C and D&C, are linked to cancer.

Snag, You're It!

Here's a chemical-free way to help preserve delicate projects like these: Prevent snagging your lace-weight yarn on scraggly cuticles by moisturizing them daily with handmade cuticle oil. Fill a small squeeze bottle with olive oil and add several drops of tea tree oil. Shake until mixed, and massage a drop onto each nail bed. A dab'll do ya!

REbooty

REbooty

There's nothing more adorable than a pair of chunky legs stuffed into knitted booties. These are made from yarn we recycled from a thrift store sweater, hand-dyed with coffee and rose petals, and made a wee bit longer than traditional booties to accentuate those luscious baby thighs.

Skill Level

Size
0–6 months

Finished Measurements
Length: 4"/10cm

Materials and Tools
Recycled, naturally dyed, worsted weight wool: in either 1 or 2 colors (A and B)—approx 100yd/91m of worsted weight yarn, **④**

Knitting needles: 4.5mm (size 7 U.S.) dpns or size to obtain gauge

Tapestry needle

Silk ribbon

Gauge
20 sts and 28 rows = 4"/10cm

Always take time to check your gauge.

Instructions

BOOTIES (MAKE 2)
Note: These instructions are for the striped version. To make solid booties, work in A throughout.

SOLE/HEEL
Using only 2 of the dpns and A, CO 35 sts. Work straight in garter st for 1¾"/4cm. BO.

INSTEP
With RS facing, count in 14 sts from the top right corner. With B, pick up and knit 9 sts.

Next row: Purl.

Join A, work even for 2 rows.

Work 4 more rows in St st, maintaining stripe pattern, ending with a stripe in A.

Using tapestry needle, seam up the bottom of foot and heel. Lay the instep in place and seam along sides—9 sts remain on 1 dpn.

CUFF
With B, knit across 9 sts, pick up and knit 17 sts around ankle (divide evenly between 2 more dpns). Including the 9 sts already on 1 dpn—26 sts total on 3 dpns. Pm at beg of round.

Knit 1 round. Change to A.

Maintaining the A/B stripe pattern, on the next round work k1, *yo, k2tog; rep from * to last st, k1 (eyelet openings made).

Work in St st for approx 3"/8cm, ending with B.

Change to A, work in k1, p1 rib for 4 rounds. BO in pat.

FINISHING
Weave in ends. Run silk ribbon piece through eyelet holes and tie.

Vickie:

I love turning thrift store "trash" into knitted treasures. Do you go thrifting at all?

Adrienne:

You know, my thrift store days have been minimal over the past few years. I dig the mileage we were able to get out of just one sweater—we used it for two different projects in this book—so I may have to reunite myself with thrift stores!

Sweater Redux

Recycling sweaters is a great way to cut down not only on waste but also on making gaping holes in your pocketbook. For about the cost of a sandwich, we got a wool thrift store sweater, and repurposed it into our REbooties and Nature Calls soakers on page 54. Here are a few tips on what to look for in a sweater to be recycled for its yarn.

- Choose a color you like. If you don't like it in its current incarnation, you won't like it when it's reknit either.

- If you plan to dye the recycled yarn, look for 100 percent wool or other animal fiber.

- Gauge matters. We've learned from experience that with a few exceptions, sweaters with a gauge of about 5 sts or less per inch seem to unwind easier with fewer frustrating tangles.

- Avoid serged seams. Turn the sweater inside out before you purchase it, and if you see serged (finished) seams, back away from the garment! These sweaters will unravel in pieces, row by row, leaving you with nothing more than a big ol' pile of scraps.

Rub-a-Dub-Dub

As cute as our booties are, there's nothing like a little barefoot time for baby. Take a few minutes of tootsie time to massage your wee one's feet and legs. Those precious moments will help nourish blood circulation and provide invaluable bonding time.

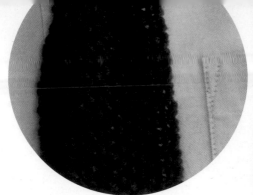

Skill Level

Size
One Size Fits All

Finished Measurements
2½ x 55½"/6 x 141cm

Materials and Tools
SWTC/Vickie Howell Collection Rock
    (40% Soysilk, 30% fine wool, 30%
    hemp; 1.75oz/50g = 109yd/99m):
    1 skein, color Joan #758—approx
    109yd/99m of worsted weight yarn,
    ④

Knitting needles: 4.5mm (size 7 U.S.) or
    size to obtain gauge

Tapestry needle

Gauge
20 sts and 28 rows = 4"/10cm

Always take time to check your gauge.

Tie-Phoon

We think skinny ties and environmentalism are both punk rock in their own right—but mix them together as we did with our hemp and soy tie, and you've got yourself some straight up greenarchy!

Instructions

CO 2 sts.

Row 1: K1, p1.

Row 2: P1, k1.

Row 3: [P1, k1 in same st] twice—4 sts.

Row 4: K1, p1 across.

Row 5: (K1, p1 in same st), k1, p1 to last st, (k1, p1 in same st)—6 sts.

Row 6: P1, k1 across.

Row 7: (P1, k1 in same st), p1, k1 to last st, (p1, k1 in same st)—8 sts.

Row 8: Rep Row 4.

Row 9: (K1, p1 in same st), k1, p1 to last st, (k1, p1 in same st)—10 sts.

Row 10: Rep Row 6.

Row 11: (P1, k1 in same st), p1, k1 to last st, (p1, k1 in same st)—12 sts.

Continue in seed st until piece measures 21"/53cm from tip, ending with a WS row.

Next row (RS): Ssk, work in seed st to last 2 sts, k2tog—10 sts.

Work even in seed st until piece measures 54½"/138cm, ending with a WS row.

Next row (RS): Ssk, work in seed st to last 2 sts, k2tog—8 sts.

Next row: Work in seed st.

Rep last 2 rows twice more—4 sts.

Next row (RS): Ssk, k2tog. BO.

FINISHING

Weave in ends. Block if necessary.

Adrienne:

Hemp: It's not just for smoking anymore!

Vickie:

Har, har, har. Now seriously…

We ❤ Hemp

• Hemp fabric is naturally one of the most ecologically friendly fibers.

• Hemp yarn is derived from the growth of industrial hemp, a different species from its more (in)famous cousin. Industrial hemp grows fast without the need for much pesticide or herbicide.

• Hemp is cool to wear in the summer and warm in the winter, and it gets softer every time you wash it.

• Hemp naturally repels up to 90 percent of UV rays!

• Hemp can grow in any climate or soil condition.

Tie Guide: A Quick Tutorial on How to Tie One On

1. Place the tie around the neck, right side up, with the wider end hanging about 12" (30.5cm) below the narrow one. Cross the wide end over the narrow end, making an X fairly close to your neck.

2. Loop the wide end underneath the narrow one, back over it, up through the neck hole, and down behind the nearly finished knot you've created.

3. Tighten the tie by shimmying the knot closer to the neck. Straighten it up, if necessary.

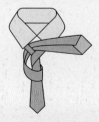

FOR THE BODY

Cardigan Neutral

This little cardi promises to become your new wardrobe BFF. Its simple silhouette goes with any outfit, while the asymmetrical lace panel sets it apart. Stitched up in delicious organic merino wool, it's so soft you'll never want to take it off!

Skill Level

Size
Women's XS (S, M, L, XL, XXL, XXXL)

Finished Measurements
Bust: 28 (32, 36, 40, 44, 48, 52)"/71 (81, 91, 102, 112, 122, 132)cm

Length: 21 (21, 21½, 22, 22½, 23, 23½)"/53 (53, 55, 56, 57, 58, 60)cm

Materials and Tools
Zitron Nimbus (100% certified organic merino wool; 1.75oz/50g = 110yd/100m): 6 (7, 8, 9, 10, 11, 12) skeins, color Charcoal Grey #413—approx 660 (770, 880, 990, 1100, 1210, 1320)yd/600 (700, 800, 900, 1000, 1100, 1200)m of worsted weight yarn, (4)

Knitting needles: 8mm (size 11 U.S.) or size to obtain gauge

Stitch holder

Tapestry needle

Gauge
12 sts and 20 rows = 4"/10cm in St st

Always take time to check your gauge.

Pattern Stitch

Foliage Lace
Row 1 (RS): K5, p2tog, k2, yo, k5, yo, k2, p2tog, k2.

Row 2 (and all WS rows): Purl.

Row 3: K4, p2tog, k2, yo, k1, yo, k2, p2tog, k7.

Row 5: K3, p2tog, k2, yo, k3, yo, k2, p2tog, k6.

Row 7: K2, p2tog, k2, yo, k5, yo, k2, p2tog, k5.

Row 9: K7, p2tog, k2, yo, k1, yo, k2, p2tog, k4.

Row 11: K6, p2tog, k2, yo, k3, yo, k2, p2tog, k3.

Row 12: Purl.

Rep Rows 1–12 for pat.

Instructions

BACK
CO 52 (58, 64, 70, 76, 82, 88) sts. Work 2 rows in St st.

Next row (RS): Ssk, knit to last 2 sts, k2tog.

Next row: Purl.

Rep last 2 rows 4 times more—42 (48, 54, 60, 66, 72, 78) sts.

Work even in St st until piece measures 8"/20cm, ending with a WS row.

Next row (RS): Ssk, knit to last 2 sts, k2tog—40 (46, 52, 58, 64, 70, 76) sts.

Work even in St st for 3 rows.

Rep last 4 rows twice more—36 (42, 48, 54, 60, 66, 72) sts.

Next row (RS): K1, M1, knit to last st, M1, k1—38 (44, 50, 56, 62, 68, 74) sts.

Work even in St st for 3 rows.

Rep last 4 rows twice more—42 (48, 54, 60, 66, 72, 78) sts.

Work even until piece measures 15"/38cm, ending with a WS row.

6 (6, 6½, 7, 7½, 8, 8½)"/15 (15, 17, 18, 19, 20, 22)cm

15"/38cm

21 (21, 21½, 22, 22½, 23, 23½)"/53 (53, 55, 56, 57, 58, 60)cm

14 (16, 18, 20, 22, 24, 26)"/36 (41, 46, 51, 56, 61, 66)cm

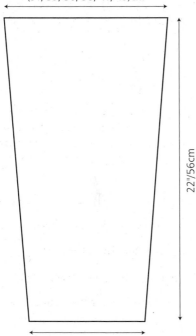

12 (12, 13, 14, 15, 16, 17)"/31 (31, 33, 36, 38, 41, 43)cm

22"/56cm

8½ (8½, 8½, 10½, 10½, 10½, 12½)"/22 (22, 22, 27, 27, 27, 32)cm

Shape Armholes

Next row (RS): BO 2 (2, 2, 3, 3, 3, 4) sts, ssk, knit to last 2 sts, k2tog.

Next row: BO 2 (2, 2, 3, 3, 3, 4) sts, purl to end—36 (42, 48, 52, 58, 64, 68) sts.

Work even until armhole measures 6 (6, 6½, 7, 7½, 8, 8½)"/15 (15, 17, 18, 19, 20, 22)cm, ending with a WS row.

Shape Neck

Next row (RS): K8 (11, 14, 14, 16, 18, 18), BO 20 (20, 20, 24, 26, 28, 32) sts for back neck, k8 (11, 14, 14, 16, 18, 18).

Next row: P8 (11, 14, 14, 16, 18, 18), leave last 8 (11, 14, 14, 16, 18, 18) sts on holder.

Next row: BO 8 (11, 14, 14, 16, 18, 18) sts.

Rejoin yarn on WS of rem sts and p8 (11, 14, 14, 16, 18, 18).
BO.

LEFT FRONT

CO 26 (28, 30, 34, 36, 40, 42) sts.

Row 1 (RS): Knit.

Row 2 (and all WS rows): K2, purl to end.

Row 3: Ssk, knit to last 22 sts, work Row 1 of Foliage Lace pat, k2—25 (27, 29, 33, 35, 39, 41) sts.

Row 5: Ssk, knit to last 22 sts, work Row 3 of Foliage Lace pat, k2.

Row 7: Ssk, knit to last 22 sts, work Row 5 of Foliage Lace pat, k2—23 (25, 31, 33, 37, 39) sts.

Work even in pat until piece measures 8"/20cm, ending with a WS row.

Next row (RS): Ssk, knit to end—22 (24, 26, 30, 32, 36, 38) sts.

Work 3 rows in pat.

Rep last 4 rows twice more—20 (22, 24, 28, 30, 34, 36) sts.

Next row (RS): K1, M1, knit to end—21 (23, 25, 29, 31, 35, 37) sts.

Work 3 rows in pat. Rep last 4 rows twice more—23 (25, 27, 31, 33, 37, 39) sts.

Work even until piece measures 15"/38cm, ending with a WS row.

Shape Armhole

Next row (RS): BO 2 (2, 2, 3, 3, 3, 4) sts, ssk, knit to end—21 (22, 24, 27, 29, 33, 34) sts.

Next row: K2, purl to end.

Shape Neck

Next row (RS): Knit to last 2 sts, k2tog.

Next row: K2, purl to end.

Rep last 2 rows until 8 (11, 14, 14, 16, 18, 18) sts rem.

Work even until armhole measures 6 (6, 6½, 7, 7½, 8, 8½)"/15 (15, 17, 18, 19, 20, 22)cm.
BO.

RIGHT FRONT

Work as for Left Front, reversing shaping and replacing pattern st with St st.

SLEEVES (MAKE 2)

Cuff

CO 26 (26, 26, 32, 32, 32, 38) sts.
Rows 1 (RS): K3 (3, 3, 6, 6, 6, 9),
work Row 1 of Foliage Lace pat, k3
(3, 3, 6, 6, 6, 9).
Row 2 (and all WS Rows): Purl.
Work even in pat for 3"/8cm, ending with a WS row. BO.

Sleeve

CO 26 (26, 26, 32, 32, 32, 38) sts.
Working in St st, inc 1 st each
end every 4th row until there are
36 (36, 40, 42, 46, 48, 52) sts.
Work even until sleeve measures
22"/56cm. BO.

FINISHING

Sew cuffs onto sleeves with wrong
sides together so that exposed
seams are on the RS.
Sew shoulder seams, attach
sleeves, and sew side and sleeve
seams. Weave in ends. Block.

 Vickie:
Global warming is one of the more controversial
topics in the environmental debate, don't you think?

 Adrienne:
I believe it was, but fortunately, because there are
now so many resources for people to tap into,
there's a much greater understanding of what we're
dealing with.

Global What-ing?

The term global warming has been (necessarily) imprinted
onto our brains over the past few years, but what does it
really mean, anyway? In a nutshell, global warming is the
phenomenon of the Earth and oceans' temperatures ris-
ing, due in large part to the excessive emissions of carbon
dioxide. Being carbon neutral—note our play on words
for this project—is the practice of having net zero carbon
emissions by reducing energy consumption and/or offset-
ting emissions with other practices, such as planting trees
or investing in alternative energy sources such as wind
turbines.

Giving = Good

Part of taking care of the Earth means taking care of each
other, and stitching for those in need is a great way to do
just that. Here are a few of our favorite fiber-related chari-
ties where you can make a difference in someone's life, one
stitch at a time.

Warm Up America www.warmupamerica.org

Stitches from the Heart www.stitchesfromtheheart.org

Warm Woolies www.warmwoolies.org

Snuggles Project www.snugglesproject.org

Afghans for Afghans www.afghansforafghans.org

FOR THE BODY

Nature Walk

Whether you're a certified nature gal who enjoys hiking trails or an avid movie fan who prefers cuddling up on the couch with a good DVD, life's little journeys are always better in thick, comfy socks. Our organic ribbed version is durable enough to wear with boots, but thanks to the pink toes and picot edges, they're still pretty enough for a girl's night in!

Skill Level

Size
Women's Medium

Finished Measurements
Foot circumference: 8"/20cm

Materials and Tools
Kickadee Nature's Colours Sock Yarn (50% young adult mohair, 32% merino lamb, 18% tussah silk; 1.75oz/50g = 170yd/155m): (A), 2 skeins, color Walnut; (B), 1 skein color Rose—approx 680yd/620m of sport weight yarn, ②

Knitting needles: 3.25mm (size 3 U.S.) dpns or size to obtain gauge

Crochet hook: 4mm (size F U.S.)

Stitch holder

Tapestry needle

Gauge
24 sts and 32 rows= 4"/10cm

Always take time to check your gauge.

Pattern Stitch

Twisted Cable Rib
Rounds 1, 2, and 4: *K2, p2; rep from * to last 2 sts, k2.

Round 3 (RS): *K2tog but don't slip off needle, then insert RH needle between these 2 sts and knit the 1st st again, slip both sts off needle tog, p2; rep from * around, end with k2tog step.

Instructions

SOCK (MAKE 2)
With A, CO 52 sts. Divide sts evenly over 3 needles. Join, taking care not to twist the sts.

Leg
Work in k2, p2 rib for 7"/18cm.

Heel Flap
Place 26 sts on one needle. Place rem instep sts on holder and continue as follows:

Row 1 (RS): *Sl1, k1; rep from * across.

Row 2: Sl1, purl to end.

Rep these 2 rows 15 times, or until flap is square.

Heel
Row 1 (RS): Sl1, k14, ssk, k1, turn.

Row 2: Sl1, p5, p2tog, p1, turn.

Row 3: Sl1, k6, ssk, k1, turn.

Row 4: Sl1, p7, p2tog, p1, turn.

Continue in this manner, slipping 1st st, working to 1 st before gap, and working sts before and after gap tog, until all heel sts are worked—16 sts.

Gusset
Set up round

Needle 1: Knit heel sts, pick up and knit 13 sts along side of heel.

Needle 2: Begin Twisted Cable Rib pat, working all 26 sts for instep.

Needle 3: Pick up and knit 13 sts along side of heel. Knit 1st 8 sts of heel. Rounds beg and end at this point—68 sts.

Round 1
Needle 1: Knit to 3 sts before the end of needle, k2tog, k1.

Needle 2: Work in pat across instep sts.

Needle 3: K1, ssk, knit to end.

Round 2
Work even in pat.

Rep Rounds 1 and 2 until there are 52 sts.

FOOT
Work even in pat until foot measures 7"/18cm or 1½"/4cm less than desired length.

TOE
Change to B.

Round 1:

Needle 1: Knit to last 3 sts, k2tog, k1.

Needle 2: K1, ssk, knit to last 3 sts, k2tog, k1.

Needle 3: K1, ssk, knit to end of needle.

Round 2:

Knit.

Rep Rounds 1 and 2 until 14 sts remain.

FINISHING

Graft toe using Kitchener st.

Picot Edging

With crochet hook and B, join yarn at top edge of sock.

*Ch 4, sl st in 4th ch from hook, skip 1, sc in next st; rep from * around. Fasten off.

Weave in ends.

Adrienne:

Vic, have you ever thought about asking people to take off their shoes before entering your home?

 Vickie:

To be honest, no, but it's a really good idea, so I may change that!

Keep Out!

Recent research shows that a staggering amount of toxins are brought into the home each time you walk through the door. The soles of your shoes act as a vehicle for things such as lawn pesticides and street chemicals. Once these poisons are in your house, they're unable to break down, without direct sunlight and they often end up circulating through the air system. This occurrence causes the chemical rate in your living space to be 100 times higher than outdoor levels! Don't worry, though—simply leaving your shoes at the door when entering the home keeps a load of chemicals out and the inside of your home clean.

R-R-R-Reflex(ology)

The key to your soul is in your sole! Treat your tootsies with our eco-friendly socks and a stimulating massage.

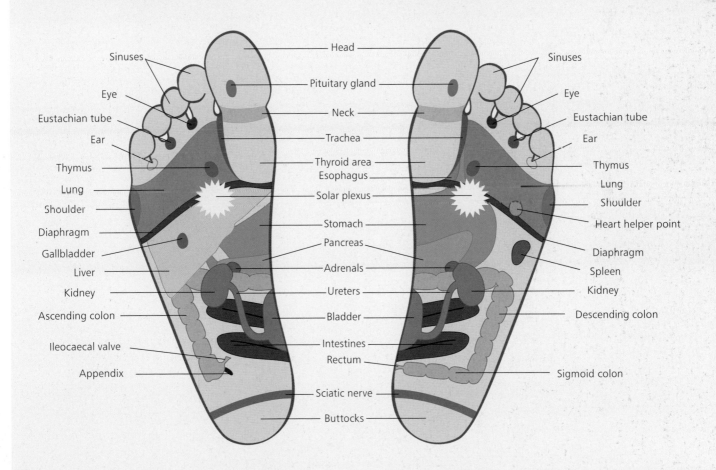

FOR THE BODY

Nature Calls

Whether you choose to go with cloth or disposable diapers for your wee one, wool soakers are both fashionable and functional. These shorties are made from thrifted wool that's been gently cleaned and hand-dyed naturally in the kitchen. They're quick to whip up and you can feel good knowing that your little cutie's clothing is free of chemical dyes.

Skill Level

Size

0–3 months (3–6 months, 6–12 months)

Finished Measurements

Hip: 14 (15, 17)"/36 (38, 43)cm

Leg opening: Stretches to fit 7 (8, 9)"/18 (20, 23)cm thigh

Materials and Tools

Recycled, worsted weight wool—approx 100 (110, 130)yd/91 (100, 118)m of worsted weight yarn, (4) (Ours are made from the same sweater that the REbooties on page 41 came from.)

For girlie version only, scraps of worsted weight wool in contrasting color, (4)

Knitting needles: 3.75mm (size 5 U.S.) 12"/30.5cm circular and dpns and 4mm (size 6 U.S.) 12"/30.5cm circular or size to obtain gauge

Crochet hook: 5mm (size H U.S.)

Stitch holder

Tapestry needle

Gauge

16 sts and 24 rows = 4"/10cm in St st using larger needles

Always take time to check your gauge.

Instructions

Using smaller circular needles, CO 56 (60, 68) sts. Join, taking care not to twist the sts.

Rounds 1–2: *K2, p2; rep from * around.

Round 3 (create eyelets): *Yo, k2tog, p2; rep from * around.

Rounds 4–6: *K2, p2; rep from * around.

Change to larger needles.

Work in St st for 4 (5, 7)"/10 (13, 18)cm more.

Next round. K16 (18, 20), place 24 (24, 28) front sts on holder, leave remaining sts on needle.

From now on, work back and forth in rows on 32 (36, 40) sts.

Next row (WS): Purl—32 (36, 40) sts.

Next row: P2tog twice, knit to last 4 sts, k2tog twice—28 (32, 36) sts.

Rep last 2 rows 4 times more—12 (16, 20) sts.

Next row: Ssk, knit to last 2 sts, k2tog—10 (14, 18) sts.

Next row: Purl.

Rep last 2 rows 1 (2, 3) times more—8 (10, 12) sts.

Work 2 rows in St st.

Next row (RS): K1, M1, knit to last st, M1, k1—10 (12, 14) sts.

Next row: Purl.

Place 10 (12, 14) sts on holder. Cut yarn.

With WS facing, place 24 (24, 28) sts on holder back on needle. Join yarn. Purl 1 row.

Next row: Ssk twice, knit to last 4 sts, k2tog twice—20 (20, 24) sts.

Next row: Purl.

Rep last 2 rows twice more—12 (12, 16) sts.

Next row: Ssk, knit to last 2 sts, k2tog—10 (10, 14) sts.

Next row: Purl.

Rep last 2 rows 1 (0, 1) times more—8 (10, 12) sts.

Work until front measures same as for back, ending with a WS row.

Next row (RS): K1, M1, knit to last st, M1, k1—10 (12, 14) sts.

Place sts on holder back on needle. Hold so front and back are parallel; graft crotch tog using Kitchener st.

LEG BANDS

With dpns, pick up and knit 28 (32, 36) sts around leg opening. Work in k1, p1 rib for 5 rounds. BO in pat. Note: For "chunkyriffic" baby thighs, use larger needles for leg ribbing.

Rep for other leg.

FINISHING

Weave in ends.

Ruffle, for girlie version only
Hold soaker upside down. With RS facing, using larger needles and contrasting wool, pick up and knit 24 sts horizontally across bottom, about 3–4"/8–10cm above crotch.

Row 1 (WS): Purl.

Row 2: K1, *yo, k1; rep from * across.

Row 3: Purl—47 sts.

Rows 4–5: Rep last 2 rows—93 sts. BO using main color of wool.

Rep ruffle once more, 2"/5cm above the first.

Tie

With crochet hook, ch for 27 (28, 30)"/69 (71, 76)cm. Fasten off. Weave tie through eyelet row.

Vickie:
Having a new baby in my home put the diaper debate back on the table for our family.

 Adrienne:
Oh man, this one is so tough and so personal. There are big pros and cons to almost any of the available choices. We just encourage people to research and make the decision that's best for their baby.

The Poop on Diapers

Out of the 6,000 diapers that each baby will likely go through before potty training, each of the petroleum-based disposables (which includes most mainstream brands) takes anywhere from 200 to 500 years to decompose. And they still contain the same toxic material that was banned from tampons in the 1980s. The debate still remains, however, over which of the other available options on the market is the most eco-friendly. Here are some facts to help you make your own decision on what's right for you and your baby:

- Cloth diapers are recyclable and eliminate the disposable diaper waste factor, but they do use a significant amount of water, energy, and time to maintain.

- Biodegradable diapers are made from chlorine-free, post-consumer materials that are more easily biodegradable; however, they still create waste and without proper disposal—ideally, they should be composted—they can still have a substantial impact on our landfills.

Our Natural Dyeing Recipe

What You Need
100yds/110m of wool yarn
2 medium pots (dedicated to dyeing only)
Alum, as a mordant
4 to 6 medium-size beets and potato peeler, for peach-colored version only
2 tablespoons (29 g) of turmeric, for yellow version only
Strainer
Tongs
Mild soap
Towel

1. Presoak the yarn in a pot of water together with 1 tablespoon (14 g) of alum by bringing it to a boil, then simmer it for an hour. Rinse it with cool water; gently squeeze it out. Set the yarn aside.

2. Create a dye bath by filling a pot about three-quarters full of water.

For the peach-colored version, peel the beets, cut them into cubes, and add them to the pot of water.

For the yellow version, mix the turmeric with enough water to turn it into a paste. Stir the paste into the pot of water.

3. Bring the water to a boil and let it simmer to steep for an hour. Using a strainer, pour the dye bath from one pot to another. This will remove the beet pieces or turmeric sediment.

4. Dye the yarn by placing it in the dye bath with 1 to 2 more tablespoons (14 to 29 g) of alum. Bring this "yarn soup" to a boil, then let it simmer for at least an hour, checking on the color periodically. (If the desired color isn't achieved after simmering for a couple of hours, turn off the heat and let sit overnight.)

5. Being careful not to burn yourself, use the tongs to remove the yarn from the dye bath. Rinse the yarn thoroughly but gently, without agitating it. Wash it with a mild soap. Roll it in a towel to remove the excess water. Hang to dry.

Waste Not, Want Not

Whether you suffer from "Single Sock Syndrome" or just always seem to have leftovers when you've finished stitching your stockings, you're bound to have unused scraps in your stash. Well, as our mothers always said, "Waste not, want not." These Fair Isle–patterned fingerless gloves utilize little bits of sock yarn to create mismatched mittens with a message.

Skill Level ★ ★ ★

Size
Women's S/M

Finished Measurements
Hand circumference: 8"/20cm

Materials and Tools
Leftover sock yarn: 2 colors (A and B)—approx 100yd/91m each of fingering weight yarn,

Scraps of sock yarn in each of 3 colors: (C, D, and E)

Knitting needles: 2.25mm (size 1 U.S.) dpns or size to obtain gauge

Stitch marker

Stitch holder or waste yarn

Tapestry needle

Gauge
32 sts and 44 rows= 4"/10cm

Always take time to check your gauge.

Instructions

GLOVES (MAKE 2 – ONE WITH A AND ONE WITH B)
Cuff
With A or B, CO 64 sts.
Divide sts as follows:

Needle 1: 17 sts

Needle 2: 16 sts

Needle 3: 15 sts

Needle 4: 16 sts

Needles 1 and 4 hold palm sts, needles 2 and 3 hold back of hand sts.

Work in k2, p2 rib for 3"/8cm, adding scrap stripes (in C, D, and E) where desired.

HAND
Change to St st and follow 33 rows of chart for Fair Isle portion. "Waste Not, Want Not" phrase should be centered on back of hand, worked on Needles 2 and 3.

Note: Be sure to twist carried yarn in places when there are more than 3 sts in between color changes to avoid long floats.

Next round
(Left Glove) Needle 1: Knit, pm at end.
Needles 2–4: Knit.

(Right Glove) Needles 1–3: Knit.
Needle 4: Pm, knit to end.

THUMB GUSSET
Knit to 1 st before marker, M1, k1, slip marker, M1, k1, knit to end of round.
Knit 1 round even.
Rep last 2 rounds, inc number of sts knit in between M1 sts by 2 each time (next round would be M1, k3, M1, then M1, k5, M1, etc.) until there are 17 thumb gusset sts. At the same time, add a scrap stripe a few rounds in.
Next round: Knit to 17 thumb gusset sts and place them on stitch holder or waste yarn. Continue knitting around.

HAND
Knit 3 rounds evenly (the first of which will close up thumb), adding a scrap stripe if desired.

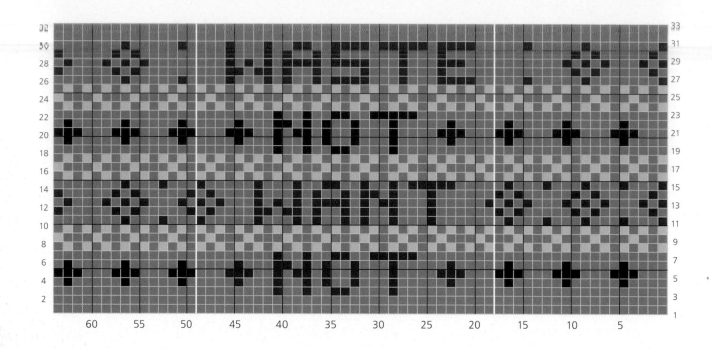

Next round: Knit, inc 2 sts evenly around—64 sts. Work 5 rounds in k2, p2 rib. BO.

THUMB FINISHING

Place thumb sts on 3 dpns, picking up 1 additional st where thumb meets glove—18 sts.

Work 3 rounds in k1, p1 rib. BO.

FINISHING

Weave in ends. Block.

 Vickie:
Do you feel guilty every time you put something in the trash can? I do.

 Adrienne:
Yes, sometimes I stress about it! The only thing we can do, though, is be thoughtful of how we dispose of things: either by recycling, donating, reusing, or composting. Tossing out should be the last resort.

What a Waste!

About 300 million tons of trash end up in landfills every year. That would fill enough garbage trucks to form a line that could stretch from the Earth halfway to the moon!

Moth-Be-Gone

To protect your yarn stash (scraps and all), use some lavender-filled sachets; they work wonders at keeping all things wool from becoming moth lunch. Sew up some scrap fabric pouches and fill 'em with your leftovers from the Green Peace eye pillow on page 94. They'll keep your stash safe, and smelling sweet, too!

Rainforest
Wrapper

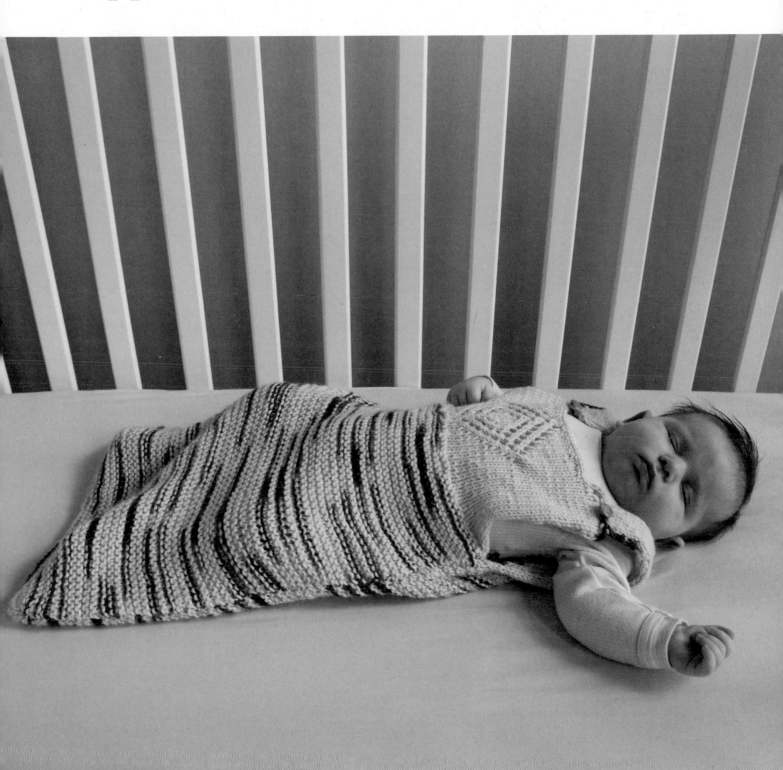

Rainforest Wrapper

Our cozy little wrapper will keep your baby safe and snug as a bug. Sleep sacks like this one are a parent's dream for peaceful nighttime sleeping, and they can eliminate the need for a blanket. They're soft, can be worn with or without a layer of jammies, and are roomy enough for your wee one to still be able to kick, kick, kick, to their heart's content.

Skill Level ★★

Size
0–6 months

Finished Measurements
Chest: 19"/48cm

Materials and Tools
SWTC/Vickie Howell Collection Rock (40% Soysilk, 30% fine wool, 30% hemp; 1.75oz/50g = 109yd/99m): (A), 3 skeins, color Ani #746; (B), 1 skein color Billie Joe #754—approx 436yd/396m of worsted weight yarn,

Knitting needles: 4.5mm (size 7 U.S.) and 4mm (size 6 U.S.) or size to obtain gauge

Crochet hook: 4.5mm (size G U.S.)

Tapestry needle

2 buttons, ½"/12mm diameter

Sewing needle and thread

Gauge
18 sts and 24 rows = 4"/10cm in St st using smaller needles

Always take time to check your gauge.

Pattern Stitch

Eyelet Diamond

Row 1 (RS): K19, k2tog, yo, k1, yo, ssk, k18.

Row 2 (and all WS rows to Row 28): Purl.

Row 3: K18, k2tog, yo, k3, yo, ssk, k17.

Row 5: K17, [k2tog, yo] twice, k1, [yo, ssk] twice, k16.

Row 6: K16, [k2tog, yo] twice, k3, [yo, ssk] twice, k15.

Row 7: K15, [k2tog, yo] 3 times, k1, [yo, ssk] 3 times, k14.

Row 9: K14, [k2tog, yo] 3 times, k3, [yo, ssk] 3 times, k13.

Row 11: K13, [k2tog, yo] 3 times, k5, [yo, ssk] 3 times, k12.

Row 13: K13, [k2tog, yo] 3 times, k5, [yo, ssk] 3 times, k12.

Row 15: K14, [yo, ssk], 3 times, k3, [k2tog, yo] 3 times, k13.

Row 17: K15, [yo, ssk] 3 times, k1, [k2tog, yo] 3 times, k14.

Row 19: K16, [yo, ssk] twice, yo, sl1-k2tog-psso, yo, [k2tog, yo] twice, k15.

Row 21: K17, [yo, ssk] twice, k1, [k2tog, yo] twice, k16.

Row 23: K18, yo, ssk, yo, sl1-k2tog-psso, yo, k2tog, yo, k17.

Row 25: K19, yo, ssk, k1, k2tog, yo, k18.

Row 27: K20, yo, sl1-k2tog-psso, yo, k19.

Rep Rows 1–28 for pat.

Instructions

BACK

With A and larger needles, CO 55 sts. Work in garter st for 14 ½"/37cm, ending with a WS row.

BODICE

Next row (RS): Change to B and smaller needles. *K2, k2tog; rep from * across, ending with k3—42 sts.

Next row: Purl.

Work in St st for 5"/13cm more, ending with a WS row.

Next row (RS): K9, BO 24 sts, knit to end.

Left Strap

Working first 9 sts only (leave other sts inactive on the needle), purl to end.

Work in St st for 3¾"/10cm. BO.

Right Strap

With WS facing, rejoin yarn to rem 9 sts and purl to end.

Work in St st for 3¾"/10cm. BO.

FRONT

Work as for back until to bodice.

BODICE

Next row (RS): Switch to B and smaller needles. *K2, k2tog; rep from * across, ending with k3—42 sts.

Next row: Purl.

Work next 28 rows in Eyelet Diamond pat.

Next row (RS): K9, BO 24 sts, knit to end.

Right Strap

Working first 9 sts only (leave other sts inactive on the needle), purl to end.

Work in St st for ½"/1cm. BO.

Left Strap

With WS facing, rejoin yarn to rem 9 sts and purl to end.

Work in St st for ½"/1cm. BO.

FINISHING

Seam up both sides to bodice.

Using A and crochet hook, sc around the entire top of the front and back bodice, working (ch 3, skip 3 sts) at the center of each strap to create buttonholes. Fasten off.

Weave in ends. Sew buttons opposite buttonholes.

 Adrienne:
Did your boys use sleep sacks when they were babies?

 Vickie:
All the time! My mom made special ones for them both.

Bath Time Baby

Make baby's bath time a relaxing ritual by diluting 1 drop of lavender essential oil in either 3 tablespoons (42 g) of whole milk or almond oil. Add the mixture to a warm bath, and your bambino's first word will likely be, "Ahh."

Baby Safety

According to the American Academy of Pediatrics, blankets, quilts and other loose bedding may contribute to Sudden Infants Death Syndrome (SIDS) and should be kept out of an infant's sleeping environment. For more information on baby safety, go to: www.aap.org

FOR THE BODY

Circumpolar Scarves

We dig scrap scarves not only because they provide much-needed waste-free relief for our overflowing yarn stashes, but also because each piece inevitably turns out to be a unique piece of art. Use our patterns just as a launching point, and play with mixing different colors and textures to create your own masterpiece; we used yarns from four other projects in the book for "Her" scarf.

FOR HIM

Skill Level

Size
One Size Fits All

Finished Measurements
6 x 60"/15 x 152cm

Materials and Tools
Bulky weight scrap yarn: (A), color black; (B), color white—approx 400yd/364m of bulky weight yarn, (5)

Knitting needles: 6mm (size 10 U.S.) or size to obtain gauge

Tapestry needle

Gauge
20 sts and 16 rows = 4"/10cm in pat

Always take time to check your gauge.

Instructions

Note: Although you have only two different colors, you'll still be working with several types of scrap yarn. Alternate them evenly for a consistent look across the entire scarf.

With Color A, CO 31 sts.

Row 1 (RS): *K2, p2; rep to last st, k1.

Row 2: Rep Row 1.
Join color B.

Rows 3–4: Rep Rows 1–2

Rep Rows 1–4, alternating colors as established, until scarf measures 60"/152cm or desired length.
BO in pat.

FOR HER

Skill Level

Size
One Size Fits All

Finished Measurements
Depends on yarns used

Materials and Tools
Mixed weight (sport and chunky) scrap yarn—approx 350yd/319m in several colors, and

Knitting needles: 9mm (size 13 U.S.) or size to obtain gauge

Tapestry needle

Note: Scrap yarns were used from Sari Charlie (page 87), REbooty (page 41), Polar Cap (page 15), and Cardigan Neutral (page 46)

Gauge
Gauge is not essential for this project.

Pattern Stitch

Feather & Fan
Row 1 (RS): Knit.

Row 2: Purl.

Row 3: K1, *k2tog 3 times, [YO, K1] 6 times, k2tog 3 times; rep from * to last st, k1.

Row 4: Knit.

Rep Rows 1–4 for pat.

Instructions
Lay out scraps in desired color order. Choose one to start with.

CO 38.

Rows 1–4: Work in Feather & Fan pat.

Rows 5–8: Rep Rows 1–4.

Change colors. Rep last 8 rows.

Continue in this manner, changing yarns after every 8 rows, until scarf measures desired length.

BO.

FINISHING

Weave in ends. Block.

Adrienne:
So, Vickie, people often have the best of intentions for recycling and repurposing, but not everyone has every resource available in his or her own town.

Vickie:
This is where we turn to the ol' World Wide Web! Now, recycling information and resources are at everyone's fingertips!

Techno Trash
Most of us have good intentions about wanting to recycle our waste. It's not always clear, however, how to go about doing that, especially when it comes to your techie gadgets. Here are a couple of great sources for responsible ridding.

For computer-related waste, visit www.greendisk.com.

You can check out a complete list of e-cyclers at http://ban.org.

Got dead batteries? Find out where to recycle 'em at http://earth911.org/recycling.

More Ways to Utilize Yarn Scraps

- Make knitted i-cord or crochet chain "ribbons" for gift-wrapping.

- In place of store-bought favors, create a variety of colored wristbands for your child's next birthday party.

- Small knitted or crocheted rectangles, seamed up the back, make sweet votive candle cozies.

- Create borders or embellishments on your larger knitted projects.

- Make small appliqués for pillows, onesies, or greeting cards.

See our project on page 112 for a clever way to repurpose your gauge swatches.

Ice Core Cap

Ice Core Cap

Whether worn while hitting the pavement with environment-related petitions or scanning for trash on an early morning beach cleanup, a beanie is what every green-go-getter needs to keep cozy. Ours is a basic little ribbed number, made out of luxuriously chunky yarn that knits up in a jiff. Activism is cool, but you need to stay warm!

Skill Level ⭐ ⭐

Size
Child (Women's Average, Men's Average)

Finished Measurements
Stretches to fit head circumference 20 (21, 22)"/51 (53, 56)cm

Materials and Tools
Plymouth Earth Collection Ecco Baby Camel (100% baby camel; 1.75oz/50g = 59yd/54m): 3 (4, 4) skeins, color #200—approx 177 (236, 236)yd/162 (216, 216)m of bulky weight yarn, (5)

Knitting needles: 5.5mm (size 9 U.S.) 16"/40.5cm circular and dpns or size to obtain gauge

Tapestry needle

Gauge
14 sts and 18 rows = 4"/10cm in St st

Always take time to check your gauge.

Instructions

[handwritten: 60 (72) 528 N]

With circular needles, CO 64 (68, 72) sts. Join, taking care not to twist the sts.

Work in k2, p2 rib until piece measures 5 (6, 6½)"/13 (15, 17)cm.

Decrease for Crown
Change to dpns when necessary.

Round 1: *K2tog, p2; rep from * around—48 (51, 54) sts.

Round 2: *K1, p2; rep from * around.

Round 3: *K1, p2tog; rep from * around—32 (34, 36) sts.

Round 4: *K1, p1; rep from * around.

Round 5: Rep Round 4.

Round 6: *K2tog; rep from * around—16 (17, 18) sts.

Round 7: Rep Round 6, ending with k0 (1, 0)—8 (9, 9) sts.

FINISHING
Thread tapestry needle through rem sts. Pull tight and secure. Weave in ends.

 Vickie:
When people think "knitting," the first thing that comes to mind likely isn't camel.

 Adrienne:
True, but because of the way their fur grows, it definitely has some benefits over other animal fibers.

Did You Know?

Camels are part of the Camelid family, same as alpacas and llamas. The members of this group of animals all have delightfully soft furs, but what's unique about camels is that their undercoat molts every spring, making them the only one of the Camelid pack that doesn't require shearing. No shearing equals no infection-causing cuts. We like that.

Caring for Your Camel (and Other Animal Yarns)

Hand-wash garments made out of baby camel, cashmere, alpaca, and merino wool in a sink filled with warm water and about a tablespoon (14 g) of organic wool wash. To prevent felting, swish around gently, taking care not to agitate. Rinse with cool water. Roll in a towel to get rid of excess water. Lay flat to dry, out of direct sunlight.

Manos Del Uruguay

Arguably one of the most successful and well-known self-sustaining co-operatives in the knitting industry, Manos Del Uruguay was founded in 1968 and is still owned today by the craftswomen who knit, dye, and spin their amazing yarns. Their soft, vibrantly colored wares can be found in yarn outlets around the world and have been used by such designer hotshots as Ralph Lauren, Donna Karan, and Marc Jacobs. Go to http://manosdeluruguay.co.uk for more information.

Rwanda Knits Project

Cari Clement (the former president of Bond America Machines) founded Rwanda Knits in 2002 by donating 60 knitting machines and training time to 100 women from tribes in East Africa. Since then, thanks to grants, donations, and Cari's determination, this knitting cooperative has grown enormously and is on its way to becoming completely self-sustaining. As a result of the program, tribes-women produce sweaters—largely for school uniforms—for fair trade, bringing the luxury of basic human necessities to their otherwise poverty-stricken communities. To get more information or to donate, go to www.rwandaknits.org.

Kidding around at Krochet Kids International.
Photos by S.W. Ramsey

Krochet Kids International

Krochet Kids was founded by three college students/friends/skaters/surfers/crocheters who discovered the extreme poverty in Uganda during a study trip abroad. Inspired to help those less fortunate, the guys recruited more of their friends to band together to create a cooperative with the goal of providing Africans with the skills to produce merchandise to sell, and subsequently nourish the community's economic growth. Now a 501(c)(3) nonprofit organization, Krochet Kids works alongside Ugandan nationals to transport and sell the group's crocheted hats to the United States, where they're sold. Visit them at http://krochetkids.org.

Oomingmak Musk Ox Producers' Co-Operative

More than 200 women from remote coastal towns in Alaska make up the Oomingmak Musk Ox Producers' Co-Operative. Their primary source of income comes from hand-knit items made from the rare and luxurious fiber qiviut. Traditional aspects of village life and Eskimo heritage influence the scarf, stole, and smoke-ring designs created by the organization's members. Village knitters mail or deliver their goods to the co-op headquarters, where the items are quality inspected, washed, blocked, and labeled. Each knitter/village is paid upon approval. Find out more at www.qiviut.com.

A Quaytu knitter.
Courtesy KUSIKUY Clothing Company

Quaytu

Quaytu is a Peruvian full-fiber production organization. Based out of the rural indigenous community Viyacocha, members raise their own alpaca, hand shear the fleece, spin the yarn, and knit a multitude of products themselves. The mill process used to produce their yarn—which is spun together with a fine Pima cotton from a neighboring community—follows all guidelines for full organic fiber.

This organization works with impoverished men and women in isolated mountain communities to bring them training, education, and income. Quaytu is being used as a model of excellence by the Peruvian government in hopes of creating countless more successful co-ops in the country. Learn more at www. kusikuy.com/knitters.html.

Fair Trade Knitters

This group of professional ghost knitters is available to produce sample garments for yarn stores, designers, and manufacturers. A cooperative at its finest, this Ecuadorian organization simultaneously fills a big gap in the knitting and crochet world while providing economic growth, an opportunity for socializing, and a boost of self-esteem to women in the Andes Mountains. For more information, go to www. fairtradeknitters.com.

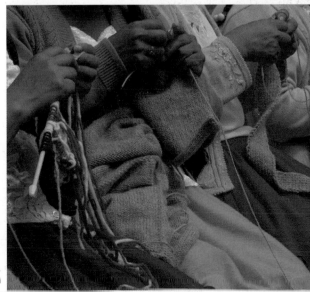

Fair Trade knitters.
Photos by Gustavo Morejón

For the Home

Home is where the heart is, and your heart longs for eco-friendly, handmade touches like soft organic blankets, raw silk cushions, lacy aromatherapy pillows, and fluffy little washcloths. Your nest never felt so cozy and fresh.

FOR THE HOME

Greenhouse

Kick plastic mats to the curb in favor of our eco-friendly option. Bulky jute rope is an affordable, durable, and nontoxic option that's a natural match for an outdoor mat. Place yours outside of your front door for a first impression that says, "Welcome to our home, green home!"

Skill Level

Size
One Size

Finished Measurements
37 x 21"/94 x 53cm

Materials and Tools
Bulky, 4-ply natural jute cord approx 225yd/205m of superbulky weight yarn, (6)

Crochet hook: 16mm (size Q U.S.) or size to obtain gauge

Large-eye tapestry needle

Gauge
1 motif = 8 1/2"/22cm diameter

Always take time to check your gauge.

Instructions

MAT CIRCLE MOTIF (MAKE 8)

Round 1: Ch 1, sc 6 times in center ring. Join with a sl st.

Round 2: Ch 1, 2 sc in each st around. Join with a sl st 12 sts.

Round 3: Rep Round 2—24 sts.

Round 4: Rep Round 2—48 sts.

Fasten off, leaving a 10"/25cm tail.

FINISHING
Weave in ends. Lay out circles in two rows of four. Using tapestry needle and jute tails, whipstitch circles together.

BORDER
Beg at the top of mat, join jute 1 st to the right of center of 1st circle (just eyeball it).

Round 1: Ch 1, sc in next 2 sts, *ch 7, skip over V space between this circle and the next, sc in 3 center sts of next circle; rep from * twice more. Sc in next 8 sts around same circle (corner of mat), ch 7, skip over V space between this circle and the next, sc in 11 sts (beg at side center) of next circle. Rep from * three times. Sc in next 8 sts around same circle (corner of mat), ch 7, skip over V space between this circle and the next, sc in 8 sts (beg at side center) of next circle. Join with a sl st.

Round 2: Ch 1, sc in every sc and ch-sp around. Join with a sl st. Fasten off. Weave in ends.

Vickie:

Even though jute may not be the softest of fibers, it's pretty impressive how versatile and affordable it is.

Adrienne:

You're right. It's one of my favorite fibers to use for outdoor projects!

Jute Huggers

Jute's pretty much a wonder fiber. It falls under the "bast" category, which means it comes from the stems of the plant, and is found en masse in India, Bangladesh, and China. It's biodegradable, sustainable, durable, and the most inexpensive of any of the vegetable fibers. What blows our minds the most though, is that jute consumes more CO_2 and releases more oxygen than trees! Who knew? Since jute is also an annually renewable energy source with high biomass production per land area unit, you can surely expect to see it popping up more often in textiles, housewares and craft stores, as awareness of its eco-benefits spread.

You Softie

Working with jute can be a little rough on the hands, so make sure to keep plenty of organic paraben- and animal product-free hand cream around. Remember, taking care of the earth starts with taking care of yourself.

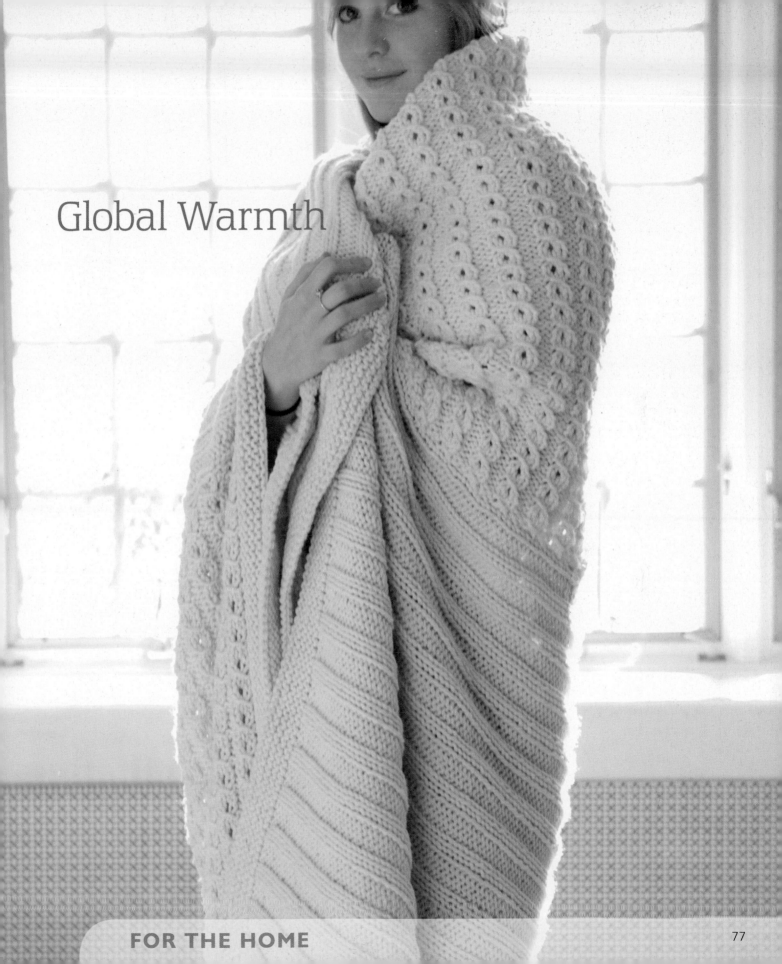

Global Warmth

Global Warmth

Although the amazing yarn for this project will cost a bit more than processed wool, the end result is a chemical- and cruelty-free heirloom you can feel good about passing on from generation to generation. Consider it a case of quality with a conscience.

Skill Level

Size
One Size

Finished Measurements
64 x 64"/163 x 163cm

Materials and Tools
O-Wool Legacy Bulky (100% certified organic wool; 1.75oz/50g = 106yd/97m): 27 skeins, color Natural—approx 2862yd/2619m of bullky weight yarn, (5)

Knitting needles: 6.5mm (size 10.5 U.S.) or size to obtain gauge

Sewing needle and thread

Tapestry needle

Gauge
12 sts and 16 rows = 4"/10cm in St st

Always take time to check your gauge.

Instructions

RIBBED PANEL (MAKE 2)
CO 92.

Row 1 (RS): *K2, p3; rep from * across, ending with k2.

Row 2: *P2, k3; rep from * across, ending with p2.

Rep Rows 1 and 2 until piece measures 30"/76cm. BO in pat.

EYELET MOCK CABLE PANEL (MAKE 2)
CO 92.

Row 1 (RS): P2, *wyif sl1-k2-psso, p2; rep from * across.

Row 2: K2, *p1, yo, p1, k2; rep from * across.

Row 3: P2, *k3, p2; rep from * across.

Row 4: K2, *p3, k2; rep from * across.

Rep Rows 1–4 until piece measures 30"/76cm.

Last row: P2, *sl1, k1, yo, k1, psso, p2; rep from * across.

BO in pat.

FINISHING
Seam 4 panels tog so that matching panels are diagonal from each other as shown.

Garter Stitch Border
With RS facing, pick up and knit 1 st for each st on bottom edge of blanket.

Row 1 (WS): *Knit to last st, kfb (to form mitered corner).

Repeat Row 1 seven more times. BO.

Rep on top edge of blanket.

On side edge, pick up and knit 1 st for every 2 rows along side edge. Work Row 1 a total of 8 times. Rep on opposite side.

Sew mitered corners together. Weave in ends. Block.

Adrienne:

You know what I find interesting about organic wool? It seems so much softer than wools that have been chemically processed.

Vickie:

Agreed. We're also big animal activists in this house, so knowing that the sheep were well cared for makes a huge difference to me!

The Scoop on Organic Wool

Organic wool comes from free-range sheep that live on pesticide-free pastures. These animals are raised humanely, are fed organic diets, and are never sprayed or dipped in chemicals. Once their wool is shorn, it's washed in a biode-gradable cleanser, carded, and spun into yarn. Knitting with organic wool will make you feel all warm and fuzzy inside, we promise!

Conscience Cozy

This blanket beauty will keep your body cozy and your con-science clear. Go ahead: Wrap yourself up in it, and bump your thermostat down. Did you know that reducing the temperature by only 2 degrees can save 5 percent off your energy bill and 353 pounds (160 kg) worth of environmental emissions? Now that's hot!

FOR THE HOME

Alter-Eco

In some states, plastic grocery bags are, thankfully, a dying breed. In others, however, trash cans and landfills are still being bombarded with these little plastic problems every single day. Do your part by transforming your supermarket sacks into reusable lunch totes. Remember, anything that can be cut up can be crocheted! *Viva la recycling revolución!*

Skill Level

Size
One Size

Finished Measurements
15 x 11½"/38 x 29cm (including handles)

Materials and Tools
"Plarn" (recycled plastic bag yarn)—
   approx 350yd/319m of bulky weight
   yarn, (5)

Crochet hook: 6mm (size J U.S.) or size
   to obtain gauge

Stitch markers

Black waxed twine

Tapestry needle

Gauge
12 sts and 8 rows = 4"/10cm in sc

Always take time to check your gauge.

Instructions

TOTE BOTTOM
Ch 4, join in a ring with a sl st.

Round 1: Work 6 sc in center of ring. Join round with a sl st—6 sts.

Round 2: Ch 1, 2 sc in each sc around. Join with a sl st—12 sts.

Round 3: Ch 1, *sc, 2 sc in next st; rep from * around, join with a sl st—18 sts.

Round 4: Ch 1, *2 sc, 2 sc in next st; rep from * around, join with a sl st—24 sts.

Continue in this manner, increasing 6 sts evenly around, every round, 11 more times. Bottom measures 11"/28cm in diameter—90 sts.

BODY

Next round: Ch 1, sc in every sc around.

Rep last round until sides measure 8"/20cm tall. Fasten off.

Shape Top

Place marker at center of top edge at front and back of bag. Place marker at left and right side edge of bag (4 markers evenly spaced along top).

*Join "plarn" at marker on front of bag. With RS facing, work to marker at side as follows:

Sc2tog, sc to 2 sts before marker, sc2tog, turn.

Rep this row 3 more times, working between these 2 markers only. Fasten off.

Rep from * 3 more times for other handle points.

Handles

Join "plarn" at top of 1st handle point. Ch across to other handle point on same side of bag. Join with a sl st, fasten off. Rep on opposite side.

FINISHING

With black twine held double, sc around the bottom perimeter of tote.

Rep this step around top edge and on both sides of handles. Fasten off.

Weave in ends.

Adrienne:
It's really encouraging to see cities taking steps toward banning the use of plastic bags.

Vickie:
I hope the use of these bags will become a thing of the past during our lifetime, don't you?

Frightening Facts about Plastic

- Worldwide, plastic bag consumption = 1 million bags per minute.

- Approximately 7 billion pounds of plastic trash floats about 500 nautical miles off the California coast, creating its own little island of filth.

- An estimated 12 million barrels of oil are required to feed Americans' hundred-billion-plastic-bags-a-year fix.

- Plastic bags are not biodegradable. It takes a thousand years for one plastic bag to break down.

- Every year, hundreds of thousands of sea animals die from ingesting plastic bags mistaken for food.

B.Y.O.B. (Bring Your Own Bottle)

Ditch those trashy juice boxes and toxic plastic water bottles! Now that you've made your own recycled lunch tote, seal the waste-free deal by packing it with a reusable drink container.

Make Your Own Plarn

- Lay your grocery bags flat and snip off the handles.

- Create a long, 1-inch (2.5 cm) wide strip (it doesn't have to be perfect) by cutting the bag into a spiral (as if you were peeling an orange). Repeat for as many bags as desired.

- Knot the strips together and wind into a ball.

FOR THE HOME

Extra! Eco!

Extra, extra, knit all about it! Turn yesterday's news into today's recycled newspaper frame. We promise you'll never look at the headlines the same way again.

Skill Level

Size
One Size

Finished Measurements
4 x 6"/10 x 15cm (see frame size listed below)

Materials and Tools
Jessica Mattingly Recycled Newspaper Yarn—approx 20yd/18m of superbulky weight yarn, (6) (or make your own with a drop spindle and paper strips)

Knitting needles: 10mm (size 15 U.S.) or size to obtain gauge

Stitch marker

4 x 6"/10 x 15cm flat front frame (with up to 2"/5cm-wide frame before opening)

Tapestry needle

Sponge brush (optional)

Craft glue

Gauge
8 sts and 16 rows = 4"/10cm

Always take time to check your gauge.

Instructions

FRAME HALF (MAKE 2)
CO 32 sts.

Row 1 (RS): Ssk, knit to last 2 sts, k2tog.

Row 2: P14, pm, p18.

Row 3: Ssk, knit to 2 sts before marker, ssk, slip marker, k2tog, knit to last 2 sts, k2tog.

Row 4: Purl.

Rep Rows 3–4 until piece measures desired height to fit frame. Since frames differ, be sure to hold your piece up to the frame as you go to get the right height.

BO.

FINISHING
Lay the two finished pieces flat with angled edges meeting. Using tapestry needle and newspaper yarn, whipstitch together. Weave in ends.

Using your finger or a sponge brush, spread a layer of glue over frame front surface.

Place knitted frame front on top of frame. Press into place. Let dry, using a heavy book on top to help keep it in place.

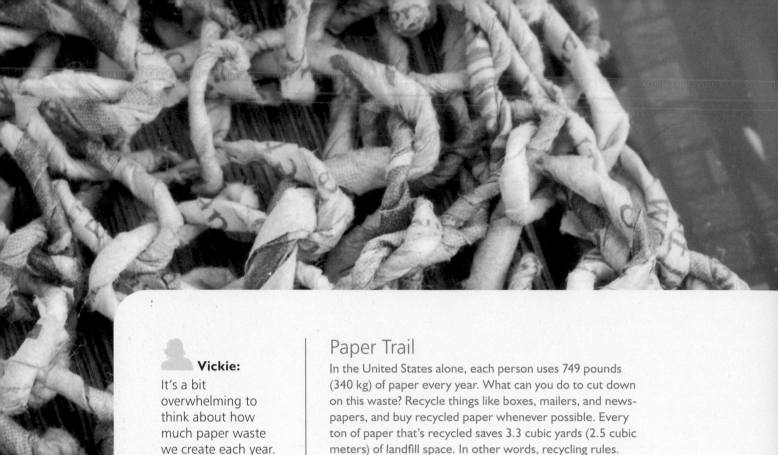

Vickie:
It's a bit overwhelming to think about how much paper waste we create each year.

Adrienne:
It's easiest to just focus on how you can recycle as much of your paper as possible, or even better, go paperless!

Paper Trail

In the United States alone, each person uses 749 pounds (340 kg) of paper every year. What can you do to cut down on this waste? Recycle things like boxes, mailers, and newspapers, and buy recycled paper whenever possible. Every ton of paper that's recycled saves 3.3 cubic yards (2.5 cubic meters) of landfill space. In other words, recycling rules.

Junk(less) Mail

Pass on the paper by putting yourself on a "do not deliver" list for junk mail. For a small fee, some commercial services will help reduce unwanted post by up to 95 percent!

Sari Charlie

Sari Charlie

The raw look of recycled silk adds a layer of texture to a regular ol' pillow. This project is not only a great accent piece, but an interesting conversation piece as well. Place it proudly on your favorite chair and share the scoop on sari scraps with all of your guests.

Skill Level ⭐⭐

Size
One Size

Finished Measurements
19 x 19"/48 x 48cm

Materials and Tools
Mango Moon Dharma (100% recycled silk; 3.5oz/100g = 150yd/137m): (A), 1 skein, color Silver Leaf; (B), 1 skein, color Lamb's Ear; (C), 1 skein, color Hydrangea—approx 450yd/411m of aran weight yarn,

Knitting needles: 5.5mm (size 9 U.S.) or size to obtain gauge

Tapestry needle

Straight pins

Sewing needle and coordinating thread

Gauge
14 sts and 20 rows = 4"/10cm in pat

Always take time to check your gauge.

Pattern Stitches

Wavy
Rows 1–2: Knit all sts.

Row 3: K6, *yo, k1, yo2, k1, yo3, k1, yo2, k1, yo, k6; rep from * across.

Row 4: Knit all knit sts, drop all yos.

Rows 5–6: Knit all sts.

Row 7: K1, *yo, k1, yo2, k1, yo3, k1, yo2, k1, yo, k6; rep from * to last 5 sts, yo, k1, yo2, k1, yo3, k1, yo2, k1, yo, k1.

Row 8: Rep Row 4.

Rep Rows 1–8 for pat.

Instructions

PILLOW FRONT
With A, CO 66 sts. Work 8 rows in Wavy pat.

Change to B. Work 8 rows in Wavy pat.

Change to C. Work 8 rows in Wavy pat.

Rep last 24 rows 3 times more. BO.

FINISHING
Weave in ends. Pin finished piece onto front of pillow. Using sewing needle, thread, and small sts, tack pillow front in place.

 Vickie:
I really love the sheen that silk adds when mixed with other fibers.

 Adrienne:
Me, too. I recently made a baby hat out of a cashmere/merino/silk blend that was AWESOME!

Is Silk Eco-Friendly and Sustainable?

Silk yarn is biodegradable, decomposes easily in landfills, and can go on to produce useful compost or soil instead of sticking around for the next 500 years, like most petroleum-based fibers. When shopping for yarn, we suggest looking for "Wild Silk" (aka Peace Silk); the process that produces this type of silk allows the silkworms to emerge from their cocoons unharmed before harvesting the fiber.

Pillow Top

Instead of buying new pillows, consider refurbishing old ones. Simply add new life with a lacy knitted front or cute crocheted appliqués. Don't you want to pimp your pillows?

FOR THE HOME

Animal Planet

Even in the age of electronic toys, there will always be room for a cuddly bunny! Keep it simple with this amigurumi pal, crocheted in the softest of organic merino wool in soothing, muted colors. This project makes a wonderful gift for the special little honey bunny in your life.

Skill Level ★★

Size
One Size

Finished Measurements
Height: 8"/20cm

Materials and Tools
Zitron Nimbus (100% certified organic merino wool; 1.75oz/50g = 110yd/100m): (A), 1 skein, color Northwest Beach #01; (B), 1 skein, color Grey #413—approx 220yd/200m of worsted weight yarn,

Crochet hook: 5mm (size H U.S.) or size to obtain gauge

Organic cotton stuffing

Sewing needle and thread

Tapestry needle

Small handful of dried beans or lentils

Stitch markers

2 small vintage buttons

Scraps of embroidery floss

Embroidery needle

Piece of decorative ribbon (optional)

Gauge
18 sts and 20 rows = 4"/10cm

Always take time to check your gauge.

Instructions

HEAD

Round 1: Using A, ch 1, sc 6 times in 2nd ch from hook. Join with a sl st—6 sts.

Round 2: Ch 1, 2 sc in each st around. Join with a sl st—12 sts.

Round 3: Ch 1, *sc, 2 sc in next st; rep from * around. Join with a sl st—18 sts.

Round 4: Ch 1, *2 sc, 2 sc in next st; rep from * around. Join with a sl st—24 sts.

Round 5: Ch 1, *3 sc, 2 sc in next st; rep from * around. Join with a sl st—30 sts.

Round 6: Ch 1, *4 sc, 2 sc in next st; rep from * around. Join with a sl st—36 sts.

Rounds 7–12: Ch 1, sc in every st around. Join with a sl st.

Round 13: Ch 1, *4 sc, sc2tog; rep from * around. Join with a sl st—30 sts.

Round 14: Ch 1, *3 sc, sc2tog; rep from * around. Join with a sl st—24 sts.

Round 15: Ch 1, *2 sc, sc2tog; rep from * around. Join with a sl st—18 sts.

Fasten off.

Stuff head and sew shut. Using tapestry needle, weave in ends.

BODY

Rounds 1–12: Work same as for Head.

Rounds 13–19: Ch 1, sc in every st around—36 sts.

Round 20: Ch 1, *4 sc, sc2tog; rep from * around. Join with a sl st—30 sts.

Round 21: Ch 1, *3 dc, dc2tog; rep from * around. Join with a sl st—24 sts.

Round 22: Ch 1, *2 dc, dc2tog; rep from * around—18 sts.

Fasten off.

Stuff body, putting beans in at bottom. Using tapestry needle, weave in ends.

Ears (Make 2)

Round 1: Using A and working in a spiral, ch 2, sc 6 times in 2nd ch from hook. Place marker—6 sts.

Round 2: 2 sc in each st around—12 sts.

Round 3: Sc in each st around.

Rep Round 3 three more times.

Change to B, Rep Round 3 once more.

Change to A, Rep Round 3 once more.

Change to B and rep Round 3 four more times. Fasten off. Stuff.

Arms and Legs (Make 4)

Round 1: Using A and working in a spiral, ch 2, sc 6 times in 2nd ch from hook. Place marker—6 sts.

Round 2: 2 sc in each st around—12 sts.

Round 3: *Sc, 2 sc in next st; rep from * around—18 sts.

Round 4: Sc in each st around.

Change to B. Rep Round 4 five more times. Fasten off. Stuff.

FINISHING

Using tapestry needle and yarn, sew head to body. Sew ears to head, and arms and legs to body.

Sew button eyes firmly onto face. *Note*: If toy is for a small baby, consider using felt for eyes instead of buttons, because they can be a choking hazard.

Embroider nose onto face.

Tie ribbon around neck, if desired.

Vickie:
As a parent, do you find it impossible to keep your kids from being inundated by corporate branding?

Adrienne:
Definitely. It's frustrating to think about how our children are such a prime market target!

Identity Crisis

According to Treehugger.com, today's kids can identify several hundred commercial logos, but only a few leaves from plants or trees.

Back to Basics

Consider toys made from organic yarn, natural wood, and unbleached fabrics as opposed to their mass-produced, plastic counterparts. They're beautiful alternatives that make great gifts and cherished keepsakes!

FOR THE HOME

Green Peace

Taking care of the Earth starts with taking care of yourself. We know what it's like to feel guilty doing anything a little self-indulgent, but just a few minutes of quiet time will make a world of difference. This aromatherapy eye pillow is a simple way to bring a little clear-headedness to your busy day.

Skill Level

Size
One Size

Finished Measurements
7 x 4"/18 x 10cm

(Note: for longer pillow, add 2 more granny squares and 6 more rows of dc. Adjust fabric piece accordingly.)

Materials and Tools
Malabrigo Lace (100% baby merino wool; 1.75oz/50g = 470yd/428m): 1 skein, color Paris Night #52—approx 470yd/428m of lace weight yarn, (0)

Crochet hook: 3.75mm (size E U.S.) or size to obtain gauge

Tapestry needle

Sewing machine (optional)

7 x 4"/18 x 10cm piece of recycled fabric

1 cup dried chamomile

3 tablespoons dried lavender

Sewing needle and thread

Gauge
24 sts and 13 rows = 4"/10cm in dc

Always take time to check your gauge.

Instructions

FRONT/GRANNY SQUARES (MAKE 8)

Round 1: Ch 2, 8 sc in 2nd ch from hook. Join in a round with a sl st—8 sts.

Round 2: Ch 3 (counts as dc here and throughout), 2 dc in base of ch, [ch 2, skip 1, 3 dc in next st] 3 times, ch 2, join with sl st in 2nd ch of beg ch—12 dc.

Round 3: Work 2 sl st in 3 dc, (ch 3, 2 dc, ch 1, 3 dc) in ch-2 sp, [ch 2, (3 dc, ch 1, 3 dc) in ch-2 sp] 3 times, ch 2. Join with a sl st.

Round 4: Ch 5, skip 1 st, sc, *ch 4, skip 1 st, sc; rep from * to end. Join with a sl st. Fasten off.

BACK
Ch 22.

Row 1: Dc in 3rd ch from hook and across. Turn—20 sts.

Row 2: Ch 3, dc in next dc and across.

Rep Row 2 for 6 ½"/17cm. Fasten off.

FINISHING
Weave in ends.

Using tapestry needle, sew 2 rows of 4 squares tog to create front.

Sew back to front, just under the chain loops to create a lacey edging, leaving one end open to insert pillow.

Make pillow insert by sewing fabric with RS tog, using 1¼"/3cm seam allowance. Turn RS out and press if necessary. Fill with mixture of chamomile and lavender (or desired herbs). Sew closed.

Place pillow insert inside pillowcase and sew closed.

 Vickie:
Sometimes I refuse to believe that stress really affects me, but when I truly pay attention to what's going on with my body I see that I'm sadly mistaken.

Adrienne:
It took me a long time to figure out that it's okay to take time for myself. Now, if I don't take 30 to 45 minutes a day for me, I can feel the difference.

Stressing Matter

Stress can cause debilitating symptoms, such as ulcers, chest pain, high blood pressure, and loss of sleep. By taking 10 to 20 minutes out of your busy day to close your eyes, repeat positive affirmations, meditate, or practice whichever relaxation technique you prefer, you can reduce some of the harmful effects that stress has on both mind and body.

Breath of Fresh Air

Aromatherapy is said to have a calming effect on the central nervous system. Lavender and chamomile, in particular, can help relieve stress and promote relaxation, so that's why we used them in this project.

Au Natural

Au Natural

Fine dining isn't just about the food; it's about the ambience and experience, too. Our citrus-colored linen place mat and coaster set will turn even a simple salad into a celebration. It's the little things, isn't it?

Skill Level

Size
One Size

Finished Measurements
Place mat: 11½ x 15"/29 x 38cm

Coaster: 4 x 4"/10 x 10cm

Materials and Tools
Louet Euroflax Light Worsted Linen (100% wet spun linen; 3.5oz/100g = 190yd/173m): 2 skeins, color Citrus Orange #62—approx 380yd/346m of light worsted weight yarn, (3)

Knitting needles: 4.5mm (size 7 U.S.) or size to obtain gauge

Tapestry needle

Gauge
24 sts and 32 rows = 4"/10cm in pat st

Always take time to check your gauge.

Pattern Stitch

Woven Herringbone
Row 1 (RS): *Yo, sl1-k2-psso; rep from * across.

Row 2: *Yo, sl1-p2-psso; rep from * across.

Rep Rows 1–2 for pat.

Instructions

PLACE MAT
CO 94 sts.

Rows 1–8: Knit.

Work in Woven Herringbone pat, keeping 1st and last 5 sts in garter st, until piece measures 10½"/27cm, ending with a WS row. Work Row 1 once more. Work in garter st for 8 more rows. BO.

COASTER
CO 24 sts

Rows 1–6: Knit.

Work in Woven Herringbone pat, keeping 1st and last 3 sts in garter st, until piece measures 3½"/9cm, ending with a WS row. Work Row 1 once more. Work in garter st for 6 more rows. BO.

FINISHING
Weave in ends. Block.

Vickie:

Would you mind sharing that awesome salad you made the last time I was at your house?

Adrienne:

Of course, I'd love to. It's a family favorite! And it will look beautiful on a table set with these place mats.

Slatat

Adrienne's family recipe for a traditional Lebanese salad:

2–3 cloves garlic
Salt
Organic romaine lettuce, tomatoes, and cucumbers
2 tablespoons dried mint
¼ cup extra virgin olive oil
¼ cup fresh squeezed lemon juice
Handful feta cheese

In salad bowl, mash garlic cloves using a flat-bottomed juice glass.

Add a pinch of salt to the garlic.

Add veggies and mint; toss with extra virgin olive oil and lemon juice.

Salt to taste and top with feta. Enjoy!

Unforgettable Edibles

Find organic and sustainable restaurants, produce, dairy, and more—no matter where you are! Log on to the Eat Well Guide (www.eat-wellguide.org), enter your zip code, your state, and the type of food you're looking for, and they'll provide a list of local eating stops.

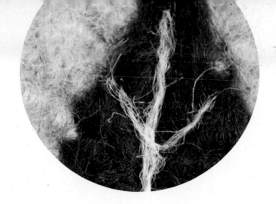

Tree Hugger

What stitch lover doesn't need a felted tote? It's a sturdy, versatile fix for life's infinite carrying needs. We added a touch of nature with a graphic, needle-felted tree juxtaposed against the industrial rivets for the handles. The result is an urban take on a classic design.

Skill Level

Size
One Size

Finished Measurements
Height before felting: 23"/58cm

Height after felting: 15"/38cm

Materials and Tools
Manos Del Uruguay Handspun Semi Solids (100% wool; 3.5oz/100g = 138yd/126m): 4 skeins, color Shale #25—approx 552yd/504m of bulky weight yarn, ⑤

Knitting needles: 10mm (size 15 U.S.) 24"/61cm circular needles or size to obtain gauge

Tapestry needle

Washing machine

Towels

Stencil diagram (page 102)

Cardstock

Craft knife

Handful of black roving

Felting needle

Foam square

4 rivets

Rivet-setting kit

2 pieces of cotton cord, 26"/66cm long

Sharp sewing needle

Waxed hemp twine

Gauge
12 sts = 4"/10cm in St st, before felting

Always take time to check your gauge.

Instructions

BOTTOM
Work back and forth in rows.

CO 8 sts. Knit 2 rows.

Next row: Kfb, knit to last st, kfb—10 sts.

Next row: Knit.

Rep last 2 rows 4 more times—18 sts.

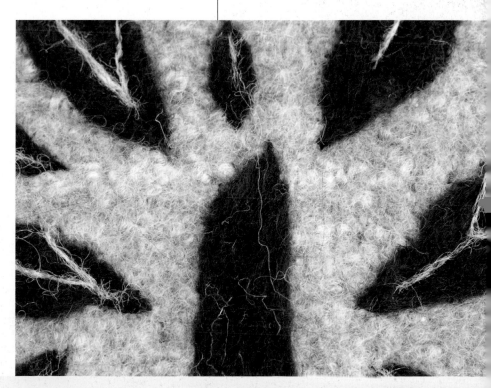

Work even in garter st until piece measures 14"/36cm from beg.

Next row: ssk, knit to last 2 sts, k2tog—16 sts.

Next row: Knit.

Rep last 2 rows 4 more times—8 sts.

BODY

With 8 sts remaining on needle (end sts), pick up and knit 35 sts along side, 8 sts on opposite end, and 35 sts along 2nd side. Join in a round—86 sts. Work even in St st until bag measures 16"/41cm.

Work in St st, inc 2 sts evenly per round, every round 9 times—104 sts. Work even until bag measures 23"/58cm. BO. Weave in ends.

FINISHING

Machine felt bag (see instructions on page 123). Let dry, stuffing with towels to shape.

Copy the stencil diagram at left onto cardstock. Use a craft knife to cut out the image.

Using the stencil, needle felt (see instructions on page 123) tree onto bag.

Handles

Following directions on package, install rivets evenly on front and back of bag.

Feed cotton cord through one of the rivets, fold over, and using sharp needle, push twine through strap and wrap around many times until secure. Repeat on opposite side, then for 2nd handle.

Enlarge 166%

Vickie:

Writing this book really changed the way I looked at wrapping gifts this past holiday season. Did you find that your awareness changed at all when you were packing your own gifts?

Adrienne:

Yes. If I didn't use fabric wrap, I tried to use paper grocery bags or recycled paper. I also used all of my yarn scraps instead of ribbon.

It's a Wrap!

Your fancy new felted tote not only makes a great gift but it can also be a cool way to present a present. Think of it as the ultimate gift bag: Next time you give a gift, consider using non-disposable options to adorn it. The recipient will appreciate your ingenuity, and the environment will benefit from less waste.

S.O.S...WATER!

Although many people in the world are only allocated 2.5 gallons (9.5 liters) of water per day, the average American uses 100+ gallons (378.5+ liters) a day, much of which goes to watering the lawn. But not to worry—you won't use nearly that much water to felt this tote!

FOR THE HOME

Simple Clean

There's nothing like an organic cotton washcloth to make your skin feel fresh and clean. We made our version with cables for a classic look, and eyelet stitches for exfoliating. Pair the smaller version with an unbleached, fluffy towel for a great baby shower gift, or the larger one with an organic soap for a holiday or housewarming treat.

Skill Level ★ ★

Size
Small and Large

Finished Measurements
Small Version: 7 x 6"/18 x 15cm

Large Version: 9 x 8"/23 x 20cm

Materials and Tools
Nashua Handknits Natural Focus Ecologie Cotton (100% naturally dyed pima cotton; 1.75oz/50g = 110yd/100m): 1 skein, color Logwood #86 OR Curcuma #83—approx 110yd/100m of worsted weight yarn,

Knitting needles: 4mm (size 6 U.S.) or size to obtain gauge

Cable needle

Tapestry needle

Gauge
20 sts and 28 rows = 4"/10cm in St st

Always take time to check your gauge.

Special Abbreviations
C8L: Sl 4 sts to cable needle and hold to front, k4, k4 from cable needle.

Instructions

SMALL WASHCLOTH
CO 40 sts.

Rows 1–2: Knit.

Row 3 (RS): K2, [yo, k2tog] 10 times, k8, [yo, k2tog] 4 times, k2.

Row 4 (and all WS rows through 8): K2, p36, k2.

Row 5: Rep Row 3.

Row 7: K2, [yo, k2tog] 10 times, C8L, [yo, k2tog] 4 times, k2.

Rep Rows 3–8 five more times.

Rep Rows 3–4 once more.

Knit 2 rows.

BO.

LARGE WASHCLOTH
CO 52 sts.

Rows 1–2: Knit.

Row 3 (RS): K2, [yo, k2tog] 10 times, k8, [yo, k2tog] 2 times, k8, [yo, k2tog] 4 times, k2.

Row 4 (and all WS rows through 8): K2, p48, k2.

Row 5: Rep Row 3.

Row 7: K2, [yo, k2tog] 10 times, C8L, [yo, k2tog] 2 times, C8L, [yo, k2tog] 4 times, k2.

Rep Rows 3–8 seven more times.

Rep Rows 3–4 once more.

Knit 2 rows.

BO.

FINISHING
Weave in ends. Block to square shape.

 Vickie:
If you had to pick one essential project to make out of organic cotton, what would it be?

 Adrienne:
A washcloth, without a doubt, because it's used directly on the skin.

A Clean Break
Taking care of yourself means not only watching what you put in your body but also what you put on it. We feel better using organic cotton for our washcloths instead of pesticide-ridden and chemically processed conventional cotton. Non-organic cotton contains seven out of the 15 most carcinogenic chemicals known to man. We say, let's pass on putting those poisons near our skin!

Soap Dish
A handmade soap stashed in your knitting bag will keep your project smelling oh-so fresh! Make or buy an extra bar to use with your earth-friendly washcloths, too.

FOR THE HOME

Buy-Locally Bag

It you're in the market for some fresh produce, don't leave home without an organic bag. Our cotton version is sturdy enough to carry loads of fruits and veggies, with a mesh design that lets 'em breathe. Make your own and say bye-bye disposable baggies, hello sustainable sacks!

Skill Level ★ ★

Size
One Size

Finished Measurements
15 x 16"/38 x 41cm (excluding handles)

Materials and Tools
SWTC/Vickie Howell Collection Craft (35% milk fiber, 65% organic cotton; 1.75oz/50g = 136yd/125m): 2 skeins, color Kelly #777—approx 272yd/250m of worsted weight yarn,

Crochet hook: 4.5mm (size G U.S.) and 5mm (size H U.S.) or size to obtain gauge

Stitch marker

Straight pins

Tapestry needle

Gauge
20 sts = 4"/10cm in sc using larger hook

Always take time to check your gauge.

Instructions

TOP BAND
Using smaller hook, ch 96. Join, taking care not to twist the sts. Place marker for end of round.

Next round: Sc in every st around. Join with a sl st.

Rep last row 4 times.

BODY
Change to larger hook.

Next round: *Ch 5, skip 3, sc in next st; rep from * around. Join with a sl st in the base of the first ch at beg of round.

Next round: *Ch 5, sc in next ch-5 sp from the round below; rep from * around.

At this point, work continues in a spiral. At the end of each round, join by working a sc in the 1st ch-5 sp of the same row.

Rep the last row 18 more times, ending with a sc to join.

BOTTOM
Ch 1, sc in next st and every ch around—approx 115 sts. Join with a sl st.

Next round: Ch 2, dc in next st and every st around. Join with a sl st.

Rep last round 2 more times. Fasten off.

FINISHING
Turn bag inside out, pin bottom together, and sc a straight seam across. Weave in ends.

Turn bag right side out.

Straps (Make 2)
Fold the bag in quarters and place 2 pins on front and back of the top band for even strap placement.

Pick up and sc 5 sts at 1st pin placement on front of bag.

Next row: Ch 1, sc in 4 remaining sts. Turn.

Rep last row for 14"/36cm or until strap is desired length. Fasten off. Join by either whipstitching or crocheting strap to top band at the 2nd pin placement.

Rep on back of bag. Weave in ends.

Vickie:

Adrienne, how have your shopping
practices changed over the years since
we've all become more aware of what
touches our food?

Adrienne:

I'm really conscientious about buying
as much food as I can that is both local
and organic. In fact, I'm pretty picky
about the foods we bring into our
home.

Farm to Market

Your local farmer's market offers a great way to
support sustainable food with its offering of region-
ally grown produce. Shopping at a farmer's market
helps small family farms stay in business, protects
land from development, and brings the freshest
local food to your own table. Many markets sell
more than just fruits and vegetables, including
meats, wines, cheeses, flowers, herbs, baked goods,
local wool, and handcrafted items. These markets
provide a direct link between the farmer and the
consumer, benefiting both.

Farmer Finder

Looking for your local farmer's market? Just log on
to LocalHarvest.org for a listing near you!

Save the Tees!

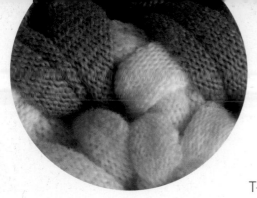

Save the Tees!

T-shirts abound in the common household, but what happens when your favorite softie looks a little sickly? Don't trash 'em; stash 'em! Save up old tees and repurpose them into an oversized basket that's perfect for holding blankets, toys, or even laundry. Remember, yesterday's trash can be today's crocheted treasure.

Skill Level

Size

One Size

Finished Measurements

30 x 13"/76 x 33cm

Materials and Tools

20–30 used tees (depending on shirt size)

Crochet hook: 15mm (size Q U.S.) or size to obtain gauge

Large-eye tapestry needle

Rotary cutter or scissors

4 rubber bands

Gauge

6 sts and 4 rows = 4"/10cm

Always take time to check your gauge.

Instructions

BASKET BOTTOM

Round 1: Ch 1, 6 sc in 2nd ch from hook. Join with a sl st—6 sts.

Round 2: Ch 1, 2 sc in every st around. Join with a sl st—12 sts.

Round 3: Ch 1, *sc, 2 sc in next st; rep from * around. Join with a sl st—18 sts.

Round 4: Ch 1, *2 sc, 2 sc in next st; rep from * around. Join with a sl st—24 sts.

Round 5: Ch 1, *3 sc, 2 sc in next st; rep from * around. Join with a sl st—30 sts.

Round 6: Ch 1, *4 sc, 2 sc in next st; rep from * around. Join with a sl st—36 sts.

Continue in this manner, increasing 6 sts evenly around each round, until piece measures 30"/76cm in diameter or desired size.

SIDES

From here, work will continue in a spiral, so rounds will no longer be joined with a sl st.

Sc in every st around until sides measure 26"/66cm in height. Fasten off.

FINISHING

Fold sides in half so fabric is doubled. Using tapestry needle and a T-shirt strand, whipstitch top edge to bottom of basket.

Snip any ends that are too long, if necessary.

Handles (Make 2)

With rotary cutter, cut 6 strips of T-shirt, each 22"/56cm long. Holding strips double, braid.

Secure ends with small rubber bands, leaving 6"/15cm tails. Poke end through top edge of basket and knot. Rep with opposite end of handle. Trim tails.

Adrienne:

Do you have an abundance of tees that you've collected over time, like I do?

Vickie:

Totally. I have several T-shirt projects on my list at any given time.

How to Make "Tarn" (T-shirt Yarn)

Step 1: Gather T-shirts to be recycled (the bigger the shirt, the better).

Step 2: Cut off sleeves and lay T-shirt flat, horizontally.

Step 3: Using a rotary cutter (recommended) or scissors, cut shirt into 1"/2.5cm strips (they don't need to be perfect). Snip each piece at the center, so that it's one long strip instead of a circle.

Step 4: Stretch strip out so edges curl in.

Step 5: Knot strips together and roll into a ball.

Five More Ways to Reuse Old Tees

1. Sew a quilt out of concert tees.
2. Knit a yoga bag.
3. Crochet a bed for your pet.
4. Grab a staple gun and recover a chair cushion.
5. Create a cafe curtain with tees and fabric.

FOR THE BODY

Swatch to Watch

If you're like us, you've got piles of project swatches piled up that you can't bring yourself to toss out. These little squares tell a story about which yarn you were into at the time, what colors made you happy, and what stitch pattern you were trying out. Pick one of your fave swatches to repurpose or crochet ours; then all you need is a refurbished frame, and a sweet display spot on your mantel!

Skill Level

Size
One Size

Finished Measurements
4½" x 7"/11 x 18cm

Materials and Tools
Scraps of paper yarn (ours is left over from the Capelet Crusader on page 34), (A)

Scraps of sock yarn (ours is left over from REbooty on page 41), (B)

Appropriate size hook(s) for yarn selected to obtain gauge

Tapestry needle

8 x 10"/20 x 25cm frame

8 x 10"/20 x 25cm piece of decorative fabric

Gauge
16 sts = 4"/10cm in dc using B

Always take time to check your gauge.

Instructions

SWATCH
With A, ch 26.

Row 1 (RS): Sc in 2nd ch from hook and to end. Turn—25 sts.

Row 2: Ch 1, sc in next st and to end. Turn.

Row 3: Ch 6, skip 4, sc, ch 3, skip 3, dc, *ch 3, skip 3, sc, ch 3, skip 3, dc; rep from * to end. Turn.

Row 4: Ch 4, skip first dc, *skip 1 ch, sc in next ch, ch 3, skip (ch 1, 1 sc, ch 1), sc in next ch, ch 1, skip 1 ch, dc in next dc; rep from *, working last dc in 4th ch of ch-6 in prev row. Turn.

Row 5: Ch 3, skip first dc, *skip (ch 1, 1 sc), 7 dc in ch-3 sp, skip (1sc, ch 1), dc in dc; rep from *, working last dc in 2nd ch of ch-4. Turn.

Row 6: Ch 6, skip first 4 dc, *sc in next dc (4th of 7), ch 3, skip 3 dc, dc in next dc; rep from *, working last dc in 3rd ch of ch-3. Fasten off.

Edging
With RS facing, join B at one corner.

Round 1: Ch 1, sc in next st and across to next corner, 2 sc in corner, sc down side to next corner, 2 sc in corner, sc across to next corner, 2 sc in corner, sc up last side, ending with a sc in same st as the 1st. Join with a sl st.

Round 2: Ch 3, dc in next st and to 1 st before corner, (ch 5, skip 3), dc to 1 st before next corner, (ch 5, skip 3), dc to 1 st before corner, (ch 5, skip 3), dc to 1 st before last corner, skip 3, join with a sl st in top of beg ch-3. Fasten off.

FINISHING
Weave in ends. Block.

Vickie:
Recycling and repurposing are important parts of an eco-conscious lifestyle. But repairs can be, too. Are you the handy one in the house when it comes to energy-saving fixes?

Adrienne:
No, I wait for my dad to come around because he's a putterer. He's my saving grace when it comes to quick home improvements.

Window Pain

Up to 50 percent of the average household's energy consumption goes to heating and cooling the home. Properly sealed windows, however, can help insulate your home, reducing the amount of energy consumed—and money spent—to maintain your indoor temperature. Here are some ways to increase window efficiency:

- Seal all edges and cracks with caulk.

- Install weather stripping in the frame.

- Hang curtains or drapes to limit heat gains in the summer and losses in the winter.

- In harsh climates, install storm windows, which help keep outdoor air from seeping in and indoor air from seeping out.

Easy Frame Makeover

Instead of running out to buy a new frame the next time you're looking for a little display dazzle, consider refurbishing old or unused ones. A simple coat of black, white, or pale blue craft paint can add a modern edge to an otherwise plain frame, while turquoise, hot pink, or chartreuse will add funk to an out-of-date, ornate version.

Basic
Techniques

SLIPKNOT

This is a basic knot that you may have learned as a kid. It's often used in knitting and crochet as a method of casting on the first stitch of a project.

Holding the short end of the yarn in your palm, wrap the yarn around your first two fingers (figure 1). Form a new loop by pulling the strand attached to the ball through the loop around your fingers (figure 2). Put the new loop on the hook or needle, and tighten by pulling both yarn ends (figure 3).

LONGTAIL (DOUBLE) CAST-ON

Calculate about 1 inch (3cm) of yarn per stitch that you'll be casting on; this will be your tail.

Letting the tail hang, tie a slipknot around one of your knitting needles. You'll now have two strands of yarn hanging down from your needle—the tail and the strand connected to the ball. Place the needle in your right hand; with your left thumb and index finger, separate the two strands of yarn (figure 4). Secure both loose ends under your ring finger and pinky

as shown in figure 5 (if you pull the needle down toward your palm, you'll see that loops have formed around both fingers).

Take your needle and scoop under the outer strand of the thumb loop (figure 6) and then over the inner strand of the index finger loop (figure 7). Let the loop fall off of your thumb (figure 8) and pull the tail so that the stitch fits loosely onto the needle.

Repeat until you've cast on the desired number of stitches.

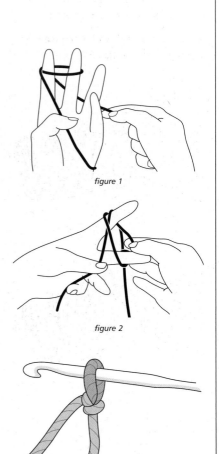

figure 1

figure 2

figure 3

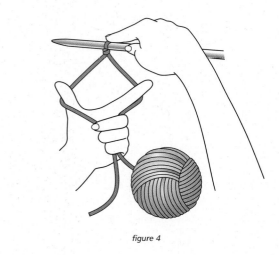

figure 4

figure 5

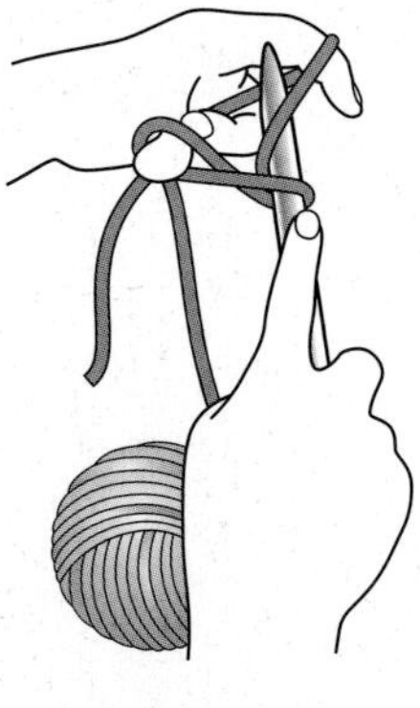

figure 6

figure 7

figure 8

KNIT STITCH

Hold the needle with stitches on it in your left hand. For the knit stitch, the working yarn is held in your right hand and in the back of the work. Insert your right-hand needle from bottom to top into the stitch as shown in figure 9 (the tips of the needles will form an X).

Use your right index finger to wrap the strand of yarn, counterclockwise, around the right-hand needle (figure 10). Bring the yarn through the stitch with the right-hand needle and pull the loop off of the left-hand needle (figure 11). You now have one complete knit stitch on your right-hand needle.

Continue until the end of the row, or as the pattern directs.

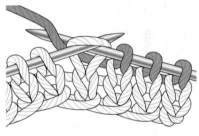

figure 9

figure 10

figure 11

PURL STITCH

Hold the needle with the stitches on it in your left hand. For this stitch, the working yarn is held in the right hand and in front of your work. Insert the right-hand needle from top to bottom into the stitch (figure 12). Use your right index finger to wrap the strand of yarn counterclockwise around the right-hand needle (figure 13).

Bring the yarn through the stitch with the right-hand needle and pull the loop off of the left-hand needle (figure 14). Continue until the end of the row, or as the pattern directs.

figure 12

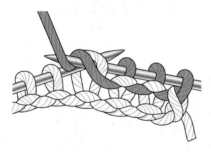

figure 13

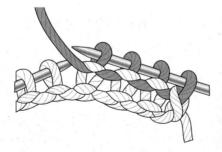

figure 14

PICKING UP STITCHES

If you're picking up stitches along a bound-off edge, insert your needle into the space that's under both loops of the existing stitch (figure 15). Bring the yarn under the needle and scoop it through the hole. You'll now have one stitch on the needle. *Insert the needle into the next space, wrap the yarn counterclockwise, and scoop the loop through the space. Repeat from * until you've picked up the desired number of stitches (figure 16).

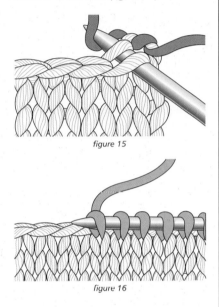

figure 15

figure 16

YARN OVER

Bring the working yarn to the front and knit the stitch normally (figure 17). This wraps the yarn around the needle, creating a yarn over.

figure 17

INC1 (MAKE 1 INCREASE)

With the right-hand needle, pick up the loop at the base of the next stitch on the left-hand needle (figure 18). Place the loop on the left-hand needle. Treat the loop as a new stitch and knit into it normally.

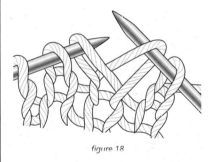

figure 18

BIND OFF

Knit two stitches. *With the tip of your left-hand needle, pull the second stitch on the right-hand needle over the first (figure 19) and let it drop off. You'll now have one stitch left on the needle (figure 20). Knit another stitch and repeat from * (figure 21).

Continue in this manner, or as directed by the pattern.

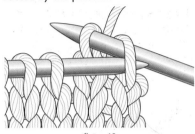

figure 19

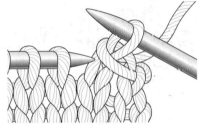

figure 20

figure 21

CROCHET CHAIN

Tie a slipknot onto the crochet hook; this will count as your first stitch. Wrap the yarn counterclockwise around the hook and pull it through the stitch on the hook (figure 22). Continue in this manner until your chain is the desired length.

Tip: It helps to hold the tail of the yarn securely between your thumb and middle finger while you're working.

SINGLE CROCHET

Insert the hook into both loops of the stitch from the row below (or in the second chain from the hook, if you're working the first row), as shown in figure 23. Wrap the yarn counterclockwise around the hook and draw it through the first loop (figure 24). Wrap the yarn counterclockwise once more, and draw it through both loops (figure 25). Insert the hook into the next stitch (figure 26). Wrap the yarn and draw it through the first loop, and then wrap the yarn again and draw it through both loops. Continue in this manner.

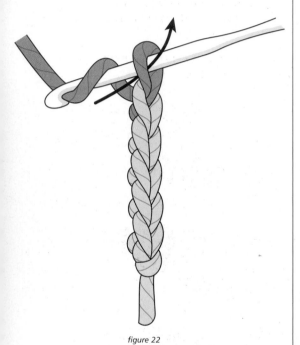

figure 22

figure 23

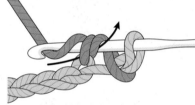

figure 24

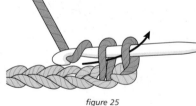

figure 25

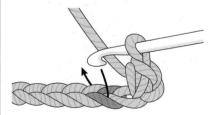

figure 26

HALF-DOUBLE CROCHET

Wrap the yarn around the hook once, counterclockwise, and insert the hook into both loops of the stitch from the row below (or in the second chain from the hook, if you're working the first row), as shown in figure 27. You'll now have three loops on your hook (figure 28). Wrap the yarn and pull it through the first loop (figure 29), wrap again, and pull it through all three loops (figure 30). Continue in this manner across the row, or as the pattern directs.

DOUBLE CROCHET

Wrap the yarn counterclockwise and insert the hook into both loops of the stitch from the row below (or in the third chain from the hook, if working the first row), as shown in figure 31. Pull the hook back through (figure 32). Wrap the yarn counterclockwise around the hook again and draw it through the first loop (figures 33). Wrap the yarn counterclockwise once more, and draw it through the last two loops (figure 34). Figure 35 shows a finished double crochet and preparation for the next stitch.

Continue across the row in the same fashion, or as the pattern directs.

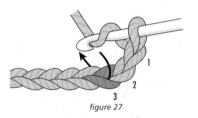

figure 27

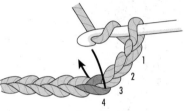

figure 31

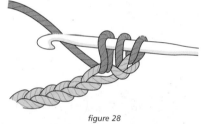

figure 28

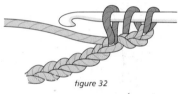

figure 32

figure 29

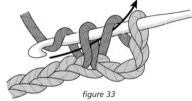

figure 33

figure 30

figure 34

figure 35

SINGLE CROCHET INCREASE

Single crochet twice into the same stitch.

JOINING WITH A SLIP STITCH

Slip the hook into the next stitch. Wrap the yarn counterclockwise around the hook. Pull the yarn through the loop(s) on the hook (figure 36).

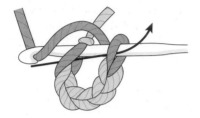

figure 36

SINGLE CROCHET DECREASE

Here, you're essentially crocheting two stitches together. Insert the hook into both loops of the stitch from the row below (or the chain stitch, if you're working the first row). Wrap the yarn counterclockwise around the hook and draw it through the first loop. Insert the hook into the next stitch (figure 37), wrap the yarn counterclockwise, and draw back through both loops.

Wrap the yarn once more counterclockwise, and draw back through both loops again (figure 38).

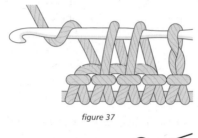

figure 37

figure 38

TIE OFF

Once you've completed stitching according to the pattern, cut the yarn, leaving a 6-inch (15cm) tail. Pull the tail through the loop on the hook to create a final knot (figure 39).

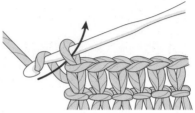

figure 39

WEAVE IN ENDS

Using a tapestry needle, weave loose ends of yarn in and out of the stitches on the wrong side of the work. Whenever possible, weave the ends in along seamlines (figure 40).

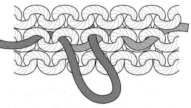

figure 40

WHIPSTITCH

Using a tapestry needle, pull the yarn up through the fabric and then come back down again fairly close to where you started. Repeat until finished, beginning the new stitch right next to the old one (figure 41).

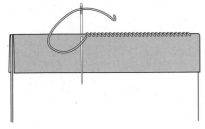

figure 41

MATTRESS STITCH

Lay the two knitted pieces that you want to seam together side by side on a table with the right sides facing up. If you pull slightly on the edge of one of the pieces, you'll notice a row of bars between the stitches.

Come up through the back edge of one of the pieces with a tapestry needle and yarn, go under one of the bars, and pull the yarn through. Repeat this step on the other knitted piece (figure 42). You'll notice your edges slowly beginning to fold inward, creating an almost seamless seam! Continue in this manner until finished, then securely weave in the ends.

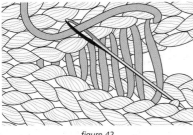

figure 42

KITCHENER STITCH

Kitchener stitch is a magically delicious way of seamlessly joining two pieces of knitted fabric using still-live stitches. It's most commonly called for in sock patterns as a form of toe grafting.

Place an even amount of front piece stitches on one needle and back piece stitches on another. Hold the needles in one hand, parallel to each other with wrong sides facing.

Using your other hand and a tapestry needle threaded with the tail of the working yarn cut after the knitting portion is finished, come through the first stitch on the front needle purlwise, leaving it on the needle. Then come through the first stitch on the back needle knitwise, also leaving it on the needle. This creates a stable beginning.

*Come through the first stitch on the front needle knitwise, letting it drop off the needle. Come through the next stitch on the front needle purlwise, leaving it on the needle. Come through the first stitch on the back needle purlwise, letting it fall off the needle. Come through the next stitch on the back needle knitwise, leaving it on the needle (figure 43).

Repeat from * until finished, stopping every inch (3cm) or so to give the yarn a little tug to make sure the grafting is going smoothly.

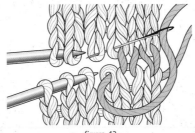

figure 43

MACHINE FELTING

Place the knitted project in a zippered pillowcase or a fine-mesh bag and toss it into the washing machine along with an old pair of jeans or a towel (this will help with agitation). Wash in hot water, but don't allow the machine to go through the spin cycle. Repeat this as many times as necessary to achieve the desired felting result, checking on your project every 5 minutes or so. When finished, squeeze any excess water out of the project, shape it per the pattern instructions, and let it dry on a towel.

NEEDLE FELTING

Place a 2-inch (5 cm) foam block inside the project, directly under where you want to add your felted embellishment. Lay out your stencil(s); once you're satisfied with their placement, use a size 38 felting needle to lightly stab a small amount of roving into place. Slowly begin adding more roving, making sure the fiber is situated exactly where you'd like it. Finally, stab the roving repeatedly, permanently attaching it to the project. Repeat this process until the design is complete.

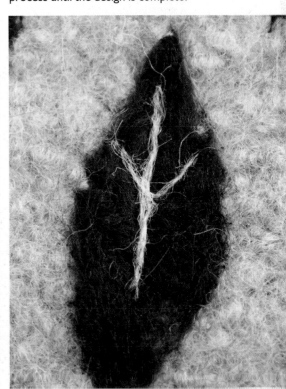

Acknowledgments

We'd like express huge gratitude to the entire Lark Books team for all of their hard work in making this book happen. We'd especially like to thank our fearless editor Valerie Shrader, whose collaborative efforts have proven invaluable; Paige Gilchrist, for a level of peace and positivity rarely seen in leadership; and Marcus Leaver, for being willing to see past the constraint of corporate opinion by placing value in vision.

We're indebted to the production knitters who helped us make our deadlines, to the talented photographer Scott Jones, who, along with Jodi Kahn styled the gorgeous photographs, and to the models who made our projects look beautiful—we couldn't have done it without you! Special thanks to Art Director Kristi Pfeffer for her fresh eco–design, and to Bradley Norris for helping with layout. Gold stars (or green stars!) to Nathalie Mornu and Kathleen McCafferty in editorial, and to Kay Stafford for production layout.

Finally, we're so grateful to have had the opportunity to work with so many diverse yarn companies that, regardless of whether they're an operation of one or a group of many, strive toward producing a product with a conscience. This book wouldn't be possible without you. Thank you!

Vickie would also like to thank:

My family and friends, whose love sustains my sanity, especially Dave Campbell, for being possibly the most supportive husband ever; Tanner and Tristan Howell, for being a constant source of inspiration; Libby Bailey, whose talents as a production knitter are only surpassed by her skills as a mom; Tammy Izbicki, for reminding me to breathe; Jenny Medford, for keeping me company via IM chats and kid playdates for yet another book; and the MEOWers, my online knitting group whose daily check-ins and advice are one of my most treasured resources. Last but not least, thank you to Adrienne for agreeing to go on this journey with me, taking me out of my color-palette comfort zone, and reminding me that simple is often better. I love you all!

Adrienne would also like to thank:

My wonderful family: Joey, Jakob, and especially my best friend, Billie Joe, who has truly shown me the path to following my passions. A big shout-out to all the ladies at Atomic Garden, who hold down the fort all too frequently. Finally, a thank-you to Vickie for her patience, talent, and weaving in of all my loose ends.

Credits

PARTICIPATING GREEN-FRIENDLY YARN COMPANIES

Southwest Trading Company (www.soysilk.com)
Blue Sky Alpaca (http://blueskyalpacas.com)
Plymouth Yarns (Ecco Line)
Kick-a-Dee Farms
Cape Cod Fibers
Habu (www.habutextiles.com)
Malibrigo
Manos Del Uruguay (www.fairmountfibers.com)

PRODUCTION KNITTERS

Libby Bailey
Trina Brielle (http://TrinaBrielle.etsy.com)
Jennifer Ancheta (http://jensknitsandknon-sense.blogspot.com)
Beth Carroll
Sue Macurdy

About the Authors

Vickie Howell is a mother, a designer, a writer, and the voice for this generation's craft movement. She hosted the popular TV show *Knitty Gritty* for eight seasons, writes a celebrity column for *Knit.1 Magazine*, designs for publications worldwide, and has written several craft books, including the upcoming *Craft Corps* (Lark Books). Her vegetarianism and concern for the environment have led her to write an eco-craft column for the health-conscious parenting magazine *KIWI*, and teaming up with SWTC to produce a limited-edition, environmentally friendly yarn line, the Vickie Howell Collection. For more information on Vickie and her projects, go to www.vickiehowell.com.

Adrienne Armstrong is a mother of two, a knitter, an environmental activist, and the co-owner of the sustainable living shop Atomic Garden, located in Oakland, California. She and her husband, Green Day front man Billie Joe Armstrong, are heavily involved in the band's collaboration with the Natural Resources Defense Council. For more information on Adrienne's store, go to www.atomicgardenoakland.com.

Skill Level Key

⭐ **Green piece (of cake)**

⭐⭐ **Environmediate**

⭐⭐⭐ **Eco-Challenge**

KNITTING ABBREVIATIONS

* or **	starting (and ending) point to repeat instructions	rem	remaining
beg	begin	rep	repeat
BO	bind off	rep from *	repeat all the instructions following the asterisk
CC	contrasting color	rnd	round
ch	chain	RS	right side
CO	cast on	sl	slip
dec	decrease	sl-w-t	slip, wrap, turn
dpn(s)	double-pointed needle(s)	ssk	slip, slip, knit
inc	increase	ssp	slip 2 stitches knitwise, one at a time, to RH needle. Slip them both, purlwise, back to LH needle. Purl them together through their back loops.
k	knit		
k2tog	knit 2 together		
k2tog tbl	knit 2 stitches together through the back loop	st(s)	stitch(es)
		tbl	through the back loop
M1	make one stitch	work even	work in pattern without increasing or decreasing any stitches
MC	main color		
p	purl	WS	WS
p2tog	purl 2 together	wyib	with yarn in back
pm	place marker	wyif	with yarn in front
psso	pass slipped stitch over	yo	yarn over

CROCHET ABBREVIATIONS

BL	Back Loop	lp(s)	loop(s)
ch	chain	sc	single crochet
Ch-sp	Chain space	t-ch	turning chain
dc	double crochet	tr	triple crochet
dc2tog	double crochet two sts together	yoh	yarn over hook
hdc	half double crochet		

YARN WEIGHT CHART

YARN WEIGHT SYMBOL & CATEGORY NAMES	0 lace	1 super fine	2 fine	3 light	4 medium	5 bulky	6 super bulky
TYPE OF YARNS IN CATEGORY	Fingering, 10-count crochet thread	Sock, Fingering, Baby	Sport, Baby	DK, Light Worsted	Worsted, Afghan, Aran	Chunky, Craft, Rug	Bulky, Roving

Source: Craft Yarn Council of America's www.YarnStandards.com

RESOURCES

These are great resources for researching your own eco-path!

www.ecology.com
www.paperrecycles.org
www.nationalgeographic.com
www.reusablebags.com
www.greenknitter.com
www.organicclothing.blogs.com
www.greenlivingonline.com
www.nrdc.org
www.eere.energy.gov (U.S. Department of Energy Efficiency and Renewable Energy)
www.massagetherapy.suite101.com
www.mentalhealth.org
www.webmd.com
www.treehugger.com
www.epa.gov (Environmental Protection Agency)
www.cleanair.org
www.greendaynrdc.org
www.ontariocorn.org/classroom/products.html
www.pioneerdays.com

SUSTAINABLE ONLINE YARN RETAIL OUTLETS

www.theyarngrove.com
www.ecobutterfly.com
www.naturesongyarn.com
www.earthfriendlyyarns.com
www.blondechickenboutique.com
http://jessprkle.etsy.com (newspaper yarn)
www.vtorganicfiber.com
www.classiceliteyarns.com
www.lanaknits.com
www.paivatar.com
www.organicpurewool.co.uk (organic wool, directly from Britain)
(See more in the Credits, page 124.)

RECOMMENDED READING AND VIEWING

An Inconvenient Truth, the Al Gore documentary
The Down-to-Earth Guide to Global Warming, by Laurie David and Cambria Gordon
Gorgeously Green, by Sophie Uliano
The Healthy Home Workbook and *Organic Baby* by Kimberly Rider

MISCELLANEOUS RESOURCES

Vogue Knitting Stitchionary
365 Knitting Stitches A Year: Perpetual Calendar
The Crochet Stitch Bible, by Betty Barnden
Askmen.com

KNITTING NEEDLE SIZES

U.S. Size Range	Millimeter Range
1	2.25 mm
2	2.75 mm
3	3.25 mm
4	3.50 mm
5	3.75 mm
6	4.00 mm
7	4.50 mm
8	5.00 mm
9	5.50 mm
10	6.00 mm
10½	6.50 mm
11	8.00 mm
13	9.00 mm
15	10.00 mm
17	12.75 mm
19	15 mm
35	19 mm
50	25 mm

CROCHET HOOK EQUIVALENTS

US Size	Metric
B-1	2.25 mm
C-2	2.75 mm
D-3	3.25 mm
E-4	3.50 mm
F-5	3.75 mm
G-6	4.00 mm
7	4.50 mm
H-8	5.00 mm
I-9	5.50 mm
J-10	6.00 mm
K-10½	6.50 mm
L-11	8.00 mm
M/N-13	9.00 mm
N/P-15	10.00 mm

Index